Beauty in the Beast

VICKI BURKE

Beauty in the Beast

Facing our Collective Shadow

BROWN
DOG
BOOKS

Published under licence by Brown Dog Books and The Self-Publishing Partnership Ltd, 10b Greenway Farm, Bath Rd, Wick, nr. Bath BS30 5RL

www.selfpublishingpartnership.co.uk

ISBN printed book: 978-1-83952-406-6

Cover Image by Terry Burke
Cover photography by Mark Brookes
Cover design by Kevin Clutterbuck
Internal design by Andrew Easton

Printed and bound in the UK

This book is printed on FSC certified paper

MIX
Paper from
responsible sources
FSC
www.fsc.org
FSC® C013604

for my wonderful mum and dad
(Julius Burke 8/6/23–28/8/16)

The Labyrinth at Chartres Cathedral

REVIEWS

"In Beauty in the Beast, Vicki Burke gives readers a front row seat on her journey of return -- to a life of wholeness and heart-centered wisdom – despite the bumpy road of these times. An essential story, the author bravely, and often with humor, explores her own multi-cultural influences and the programming that silenced her voice and constricted her breathing. In so doing, she invites readers to face their own shadowy minotaurs.

Set against a backdrop of finding kinship and belonging in the beautiful Medieval town of Frome, Vicki Burke's synchronistic and often mystical experiences teach us what's possible when we make a pilgrimage into the Labyrinth and experience its magic.

With original songs that are luminous and lyrical, it is clear that Vicki Burke has reclaimed her true note."

Jennifer A. Comeau, Founder, Sanctuary at Sunrise Hill and TreeSisters US Board Chair.

"Musician, activist and spiritual explorer Vicki Burke offers us a strikingly original, intimate and eloquent account of her journey as a Jewish person into the mystical heart of the Christian labyrinth, accompanied by her personal minotaur, a brilliant device. She invokes a remarkable breadth of cultural references and life experiences. An insightful and inspiring read."

Simon Keyes, Professor of Reconciliation and Peacebuilding, University of Winchester.

ABOUT THE AUTHOR

Vicki Burke was born in Bristol, England and lives in the Somerset market town, Frome. Her life as a saxophonist and music teacher began to expand in the millennium as she found a new path to walk as a healer. Having added harpist, singer/ songwriter, author, playwright, film maker and reconciliation worker to her list of skills, she has arrived at the conclusion that these titles become increasingly irrelevant as they are just some of the many games that we all can play as we grow and become whole.

This book is about her journey so far.

Other works by Vicki Burke

Journey to the Golden City: Finding our Way Home
Return to the Golden City a reconciliation play and film

ACKNOWLEDGEMENTS

There are many people to thank and words really don't say enough, but here goes.

Firstly, I want to thank Johanna van Fessem, my editor, for her skill, deep knowledge and encouragement.

A huge thank you to my family for their lifelong support and love and to everyone in this story who has given me permission to include them and the part they played here. This has given my tale more colour and realism.

Thank you to Mark Brookes, my wonderful partner, for keeping me grounded and for his editing skills and photography. Thank you to Terry Burke for her beautiful artwork and also Louise Chalice for her inspiration. I also wish to thank David Tanner and Jennifer Comeau for their guidance. Thank you to all the people in this book who have shaped this story and agreed to be mentioned here, and not forgetting all the other countless people not mentioned in this book who have helped me on my path.

In memory of Margaret-Mary
who died suddenly 20/12/21. M was at the dynamic and vital heart of the Frome Friends of Palestine for many years.

CONTENTS

PROLOGUE

PACKING MY BAGS

Beauty In The Beast

Hey you, you've broken in two,
Now you've reached a fork in the road.
You cast out the shadows and turned from the light,
Now you carry a heavy load.

You slay your demons and left them for dead,
But you never let them go.
Out of sight but not out of mind
Now you watch their shadows grow.

Now you want a rose without a thorn and a bee without a sting,
But an eye without a storm,
can't see the glory the breaking clouds bring.

Who will cast the judgement, between the sinner and the priest?
Look for the beast within the beauty and the beauty in the beast.
Yeah, the beauty in the beast.

Hey you, you've woken anew as the walls of judgement fall.
Your heart is wide open, your mind set free,
Now you're rising to the call.

Now you love the lion for its roar and the snake for its bite,
For they hold the key to the door, that let in the light.

Who will point the finger,
at those that famine or those that feast?
Look for the beast within the beauty and the beauty in the beast.
Who are the righteous, those that live for war or fight for peace?
Look for the beast within the beauty and the beauty in the beast.
Yeah, the beauty in the beast.

I sense it's time to pick up my pen again. I've not engaged in any serious writing for a while now as I've been busy doing other things. Over the years I have learned to put my creativity in a few different areas, all of which I can now honestly say bring me joy. I can flit from one to another quite easily and just let the universe be my guide, pointing me to where I need to put my attention next. So, here I am, once again hoping to cast my ideas, create something that might have some value.

My vision of the universe, an infinite entity, made up of circles within circles, worlds within worlds, keeps my life in motion, my mind in overdrive and my heart open. I know I have come a long way and though I can still see the beginning very clearly, keeping the spiralling energy of the feminine and masculine in balance within me, moves me forward with relative ease. These cycles of life show me that although I've completed half a century in Earth years the reality is that time is like an elastic band and feelings can bring me back to a childhood memory in a second.

I believe I have a nose for personal investigation and although it often takes a while, I usually manage to get a clear picture of my truth eventually. It's like cleaning a mirror. It's a slow, sometimes painful process but important and cannot be rushed nor can any of it be skipped. I am also fully aware that this process is only possible with the full intervention of my guides. I will speak more of them throughout these pages.

Each unfolding image brings me joy, to see myself in all my naked truth, the beautiful and the ugly. What needs healing then becomes very clear, as long as I'm willing to take the plunge. I love using these analogies and I hope you are growing your own tool kit to bring with you on your journey. Doing the work, sweeping the floor and keeping the images clean has helped me get to my next destination the best way I know how.

I see the universe as a set of Russian dolls. From a particle to an atom, from a human egg cell to a human being, to the human race, from the Earth to our solar system, our galaxy, and the universe itself. Each being, in its own dimension, is a reflection of all the others and each hold the wisdom contained in that initial singularity, the Big Bang. Just as the first cells of the baby divide again and again still holding the DNA from the original egg and sperm cell, so each conscious living being is, simultaneously, apart from and a part of the whole.

As I have come to understand how life can be viewed through this idea of the mirror, so I wish to tell this story.

When I moved to Frome in 2013, I was amazed how quickly I sensed that my experiences here, as they unfolded, were revealing many truths about my life. In a way I felt that I had stepped into a field of magical synchronicity; an experience not unknown to me. Within two years of arriving I knew I needed to begin writing my story and I will be concentrating on just these few years of my life, approximately seven turns of our beautiful planet's orbit round the sun, as a reflection of my life as a whole. I would like to also map this alongside the journey of the human race over the last few astrological, galactic months (a galactic month being 2,000 years).

Born into a Jewish family, I remained an atheist until an epiphany, at the age of thirty-two, brought all manner of beautiful experiences into my life. Ten years later, in 2008 I was gifted an astrology course, not one that taught me how to be an astrologer, but one that investigated the wisdom living astrology can offer our lives day to day. It was called 'The Alchemical Journey' created and facilitated by the astrologer, John Wadsworth. The concept of alchemy, of turning lead into gold, has been close to my heart ever since. The analogy that our hearts are golden but we have encased them in lead is, I believe, a beautiful one and to reveal the gold beneath is simply a case of letting go or turning the key on the lock. When we realise that we have built our lives on so many beliefs that do not serve us, we can choose to release ourselves from these beliefs and remember our true story.

Another take on this is the story of *The Alchemist*, the Hero's Journey, that reveals how you have to journey away from home and jump through the necessary hoops before you are ready to return, discovering that everything you were looking for was always there, but you had to leave to be able to discover this.

My musical journey: *Keys to the Golden City*, my book: *Journey To The Golden City* and my play: *Return To The Golden City* are all direct products of these investigations and I have created this book and accompanying CD as the second part in my trilogy.

What I am hoping to do here, is use the symbolism of the labyrinth to give my story a vessel in which to hold it. I have five planets in Pisces, a very watery and potentially chaotic existence, which up until a few years ago, strangely enough, lacked flow. One of those planets is Saturn. Saturn represents boundaries, death being the ultimate physical boundary, as it is the outermost planet visible to the naked eye. (It was considered the most distant planet in our solar system until about 200 years ago the telescope discovered there were more.) It therefore holds a fatherly role over the inner planets. Saturn is our teacher and guide. Learning to understand its rules became a major breakthrough and in return Saturn has offered me many beautiful gifts, cups into which to put my learning. The labyrinth, as a mechanism to shape this journey, is one such gift which I am hoping to use to help us reach a deeper understanding of the extreme conflicts we experience in our society today and how we got here.

The labyrinth was an ancient structure originally built by King Minos to imprison the mythical Minotaur. This Minotaur was a creature, half-man, half-beast, born out of the King's arrogance and disrespect for the gods. Minos had prayed to the gods for a bull to appear out of the sea, to show his authority to become king over his brothers. However, once he had the bull and the crown, he refused to honour his vow of sacrificing the bull once it appeared, as requested by Poseidon. When Minos, already consumed by his newly acquired power, kept the majestic bull for himself, Poseidon punished him by instilling a passion in his wife, Pasiphae, for the bull.

The queen called on a craftsmen, asking him to build her a wooden cow which she could hide in, and had it wheeled into the meadow to seduce the bull. The result was the Minotaur, called Asterion, who as he grew became unmanageable. Minos ordered the craftsman to build the labyrinth for his part in helping his wife realise her divinely, accursed, bestial desires. And there the Minotaur lived, regularly receiving a sacrifice of youths to appease his ceaseless insatiability.

What an amazing story. We don't write them like that anymore, filled with tragedy and metaphor.

The labyrinth was a multicursal structure, meaning that it had many routes in and out, like a maze. Once you were entwined within its meandering pathways, there was no way for the youths or the Minotaur to find their way out. Being devoured by the beast within was your only exit route. This was until Theseus fell in love with Ariadne, daughter of King Minos, who gave him a reel of golden thread. Once in the labyrinth he was able to slay the Minotaur and use the thread to find his way out again.

I love the fantastical element to these Greek myths and indeed many other ancient stories. I worry that many get ignored and derided because people find it hard to believe in them. I feel that we forget to look at these stories for their symbolism, spending too much time trying to ascertain whether they are true or not. This is very much part of our modern nature as we slip more into a logical way of thinking (ironically passed down to us by the Greeks), losing the use and importance of metaphor and also, sadly, our sense of humour, as neither aspects have a place in logic.

What the Minotaur symbolises for me – being born out of so many disturbing aspects of our human nature – is the shadow within us all. It is my belief that we are beings, living in a dualistic world, made up of opposites: masculine and feminine; positive and negative, dark and light, neither of which are good or bad, they just are. I feel it is important to note that I believe the shadow aspects of ourselves develop when we fail to find balance within this dualistic state and fall between the cracks. The differentiation between the dark and the shadow aspects of ourselves are important here and something I shall be examining more closely throughout this book.

How we view this is up to us. The theories our quantum physicists are asking us to conceptualise, such as Schrödinger's cat[1], mirror what the ancient sages have been saying for millennia. We are being shown that we are living in a subjective world and everything we experience is caused by, and the effect of, our participation in it. As we begin to integrate this revelation it feels important to remember that our participation either comes from a place of fear or love, and that fear is only a lack of love. It is in the place of fear that we often become judgemental and this often lacks discernment. When we find ourselves running away from death, femininity or pain out of fear and a belief that they are bad, we can see where we have lost our way; the shadows we have cast on our society.

Freeing ourselves from judging these concepts is, I believe, the key to life, to peace. Finding the gold in our hearts is our prize for attaining this freedom and I do feel this has, and will always be, my whole life's journey. I know I am not alone here and just the fact that you are reading this comforts me in this knowledge.

Using the labyrinth as a tool to work through my healing process only became obvious when I learned about the next stage of its existence. I discovered that the labyrinth was taken up by the early Christians. Now that the Minotaur, the dark shadow that lurked within, had been symbolically removed, its purpose had changed.

However, it is easy to see, in hindsight, how 'slaying the dragon' doesn't actually remove it from our lives; it just temporarily puts it out of sight. This is something I believe is the most dangerous aspect of dealing with our shadow as we completely ignore the fact that we have been left, symbolically, with blood on our hands. We thought, and indeed still think, that slaying the dragon was the answer, believing ourselves, like Theseus, to be the heroes of the story. The reality, for me, is that this is the furthest from the truth. I was to learn this lesson for myself.

The early Christians played a very important role in helping us to understand this complex and prolonged lesson, one we are still learning. They began to use the labyrinth as a unicursal structure, one that had only one path into the heart and one out. Not having to worry about physically losing your way, it took you there as long as you kept walking. This enabled the participant to enter and remain in a meditative state of mind for the whole experience. The intention was to ask a question as you entered, so that on reaching the heart of the labyrinth, an answer would often be received, either then and there or later. This was a powerful process of divination.

Labyrinths were built all over Europe, varying in size and style but they all offered the same opportunity of stepping into your heart and gaining some inner guidance, before gradually being removed from churches over the centuries.

In the centre of the labyrinth, clearly seen at Chartres Cathedral, just before you reach its heart, you find six petals. It is thought that the early Christians used these petals to meditate on the six parts of the Lord's Prayer.

The more I read about this and the interpretations offered the more I realised that this was a journey I could relate to. I had arrived at a stage in my life where I could no longer ignore certain aspects of my spiritual path. My relationship with my Judaism and my new relationship with the teachings of Jesus Christ, as a thing separate from the Christian Church, were throwing up all kinds of conflicts for me. This was something I clearly needed to work through.

The labyrinth was offering me a mechanism and I knew that I could use these six petals with their prayers or mantras as a structure, using one for each chapter, for this book. I sensed Saturn showing up, helping me once more.

In 2012, I met my new partner, Mark, and that summer we decided to take a trip to France. On the way home we stopped off in Chartres as we had heard that there was a labyrinth well worth visiting. In fact it is one of the most famous in Europe and still in perfect condition. We were excited to hear that one day a week, the chairs were peeled back to reveal this beautiful structure, laid into the stone over the main area of the cathedral, allowing its congregation to walk this sacred pilgrimage journey. The fact that this important tool had been removed from our culture, in recent centuries, fascinates me. I saw the chairs that cover the labyrinth, the enormous scale of it making it hard to see, as an analogy of our blindness when it comes to seeing the Minotaur, or indeed G-d. This reflects how subtly truths can be veiled from us.

I know there is no coincidence that as so many people are now crying out for this wisdom to be revealed to us, in all its vastness and beauty, the Church is opening its doors in response. Whether we wish to embrace what we find is up to us.

The fact that this ancient form of meditation is being welcomed back into the Church, metaphorically peeling back the chairs, feels like a powerful synchronistic return I, and so many others, have longed for.

Why has the Church kept this beautiful tool hidden from its congregation and removed this teaching from its practices? I feel the last eight centuries have shown how we have been kept in the dark in many ways, kept out of the gates of our golden city. While I feel it is important not to judge something to be good or bad, I will suggest that this has certainly been difficult.

It is my view that this is simply a path we, as a culture, have taken, into the shadow, so that we can choose to step back into the light. I see life as a series of lessons, we have to make mistakes in order to learn from them. It is also a series of inevitable cycles and I believe, we are probably now just entering our darkest hour, which, when we think of the dawn, comes just before the light. It is my understanding that many of the indigenous peoples of this planet, and many others who have opened their eyes to their own, inner wisdom, believe that this is the last moment before we choose to recognise that we are still living outside of the walls of our golden city. The golden city is a term taken from the Book of Revelation and symbolises our heart and our return to living by its wisdom, embraced in love. (I was inspired to use this concept in my work by a book called *The Golden City* by Chrissy Philp that I discovered while attending the astrology course.)

We have been living so far from its boundaries that we have forgotten it was there, but now, I feel, the beautiful golden temple roofs are in sight and the longing to return is being felt in the pit of our stomachs and the depths of our hearts. I know I feel it and I am running to the gates even though I know I do not have all the keys to let myself in as yet. There are no set rules to how many keys you may need but I sense you'll know when you have enough. I found the ones I needed to get me here so far and if I keep working, keep cleaning the dirt off my treasure hunt map, and digging deep, I hope to have all the ones I require to open the door.

It has been a joy travelling along this bumpy road and I sincerely hope that you have enjoyed your life journey this far too. If you have not, I would like to stress that joy is an important addition you might like to add to your keyring and if it is not one you have you might wish to make that your next pilgrimage.

You might find that a walk in the labyrinth is just the tool you need and you could try asking Saturn to accompany you. Labyrinths became replacements for those who could not walk distances as you would for a pilgrimage. It is the intention with which you walk it that is important and the right intention will bring forth the right gift.

May I wish you bon voyage, whether you choose the inner, the outer journey or both?

CHAPTER ONE

THE FIRST PETAL: FAITH

Our father who art in heaven, hallow'ed be thy name

Faith

Wake up you sleepy head.
Open your eyes, see the way ahead.
I know you're feeling warm and safe.
But blinds need lifting and minds need shifting
And our only guide is our faith.

Have you ever held something in your hand so close to the end
Like a castle in the sand with the tide creeping in?
Did you want to bring them back from the edge
Like a jumper on the ledge, doesn't know they're sleeping?

I'm a woman with love in my heart
So much to give to give, but don't know where to start
In a world that's dying.
I'm a woman with faith in my soul
that we can stop this crazy train if we let go control,
So we can start flying.

Just one step for this human nation
a leap of faith will be
Our salvation, now I believe, I believe.

Have you ever held someone in your heart
So deep in your soul you couldn't bear to part?
But you feel the tide coming in.
Did you want to bring yourself back from the brink
You know the way ahead you'll swim or sink?
But you feel it's summoning you on.

I'm a woman with love in my heart
So much to give to give, but don't know where to start
In a world that's dying.
I'm a woman with faith in my soul
that we can stop this crazy train if we let go control
So we can start flying.
Faith keeps my soul from crying
Faith keeps me strong, keeps me carrying on.

PART 1

Whenever we decide to go on a journey, whether it's on a pilgrimage or just to the shops we never really know where it might take us. It can be useful to set an intention, maybe you might want to remember to put a compass in your bag, but I've found it helps not to set a fixed outcome for that would be very limiting.

Pilgrimages can take many forms and in these busy times, finding a way to achieve the most effective outcome with the least energy, we may think only belongs to the modern lifestyle. But even in mediaeval times the rich would pay others to go to the Holy Land to have their sins absolved for them; an ancient form of offsetting your 'sin' footprint. A less expensive solution would be to walk a labyrinth, a small contained exploration that you could take in your back garden if you wished. And if you find that too time-consuming you could even try a finger labyrinth. This is a miniature version, the size of a dinner plate, which invites you to trace the path with your finger.

Another solution to time-limiting issues would be to go nowhere at all but simply imagine you are walking the path. To many, I guess this would seem like the most ridiculous, but perhaps we are living the most ridiculous of times. I have walked many journeys, inward and out, over the years, and in my search for answers, I have found that the more outlandish the postulation, the furthest from logic, the more likely I will hit the mark. And the more fun is likely to be had. The expression 'never in my wildest dreams …' comes to mind.

I believe our imagination has the potential to be one of our greatest assets. I believe that when we wake up to the idea, as some already have, that time is both linear and stationary, and allow our imagination to run with this, I sense that we might be able to wield magic?

I understand that memory, being a picture or information that we hold in our mind, does not have to work in one direction only. It is possible that we can move freely forward and backward through our memory banks as our mind chooses. Our third dimensional understanding of the world makes us think that we have no effect on the future and can only know the past, yet we are continually influencing what is to come with the images of our thoughts and fears that we create in our minds first and then make manifest. Think what we could do if we really woke up to this fact and decided to change our story.

There are many people who know this and have already taken the human race to places it could previously never have imagined going. I love the comment that Jim Lovell made after returning from the moon. He said, 'It's not a miracle, we just decided to go'.

I am not a scientist, but I understand some basic principles; the idea that like attracts like; what we are in the world we continue to bring into the world. You can't find happiness or love, they aren't commodities you can buy, they are choices we make and once we choose to feel joy or to be love, then we bring it in, affirming what we are already putting out.

So as I get ready to begin this inner journey, I am preparing to create some magic. Even though I have been working in this way for twenty years now, I am still aware that there are many pitfalls to trip me up. I am going to be mindful of staying in the moment, rather than listening to the old stories that keep popping into my head. These entrenched thought patterns are hard-wired into our ways of thinking, leaping into reaction far quicker than our conscious thoughts and keep us stuck in our ways.

These thought patterns are embodied by my Minotaur and it is my intention to bring it in from the shadows and face every aspect of it from the bestial to the beauty. I am also keeping the pronoun of 'it' because I have no idea if it has gender. Being always thought of as masculine is an issue when I am a woman. However, we have both genders within us and my Minotaur, I hope, will help me unite the two into a sense of wholeness and unity.

My first step, in my meditation process, is purposeful and confident, and takes me on a path of concrete and stone. However, very quickly I am able to rewild my mind and my toes are soon tingling with the sensation of soft grass and wild flowers. I take a deep breath, the sun is warm on my face and the smells and sounds are sweet. I am walking slowly, taking it all in, sauntering, connecting with the earth. The labyrinth up ahead is marked out gently in the grassy carpet of the natural landscape.

Before I enter I request permission from the guardians of the labyrinth and set my intention. A flicker in the play of light dances behind me and I sense the presence of my Minotaur. Immediately I can feel myself step into fear. I quell the sensation quickly, for it's not even formed into a thought, just a feeling. I replace it with a blessing and an offer of love and gratitude for myself and the complex web of magic present here.

I enter the labyrinth and am soon lost in the meanderings of the seemingly meaningless patterns I am imprinting in the grass. I don't know how long it is before I arrive at the first petal, my mind calm and connected.

This is the petal of Faith and the portion of the Lord's Prayer, that we are asked to contemplate here, I hear like a whisper: *Our father, who art in heaven, hallowed be thy name.*

These words bring a feeling of expansion, like a backdrop raised on a stage, into the depths of darkness. The more I look into this hall of mirrors, everything I believe to be clear and certain, simply falls away into the unknown.

I am brought back to the place where this feels most uncomfortable, where my shadow is at its blackest, my faith at its weakest.

*   *   *

'Who are you trying to fool?'

'I'm sorry?' I call into the darkness.

'Our father, hallowed be thy name. I presume you're joking?'

'Oh it's you.' I feel my muscles tense. I can only see the shadow of the horned beast standing close enough so I can see how huge it is but far enough away to get a hold on the feeling of overwhelm. I remind myself I have made this choice to face my fears and the Minotaur that embodies them. It's taken me a long to time to be ready for this but now I'm here, I feel a little freaked out, but, the Minotaur is just me, after all.

'You recall your mocking remarks, "faith is for people who are lost. People create a G-d when they can't bear the "not knowing", people who generally need a crutch to get them through life."' It almost spits the words at me.

I feel them land, not feeling ashamed but, let's say, uncomfortable. I need to keep my wits about me. 'I know, I remember saying those same words to my friend, my Christian friend, around my kitchen table.' I must have been all of sixteen, so confident in my beliefs, or rather disbeliefs.

'But you did join the Young People's Fellowship, at your local Baptist Church and all you did was criticise them.'

'No, well, I did, but I'd like to call it healthy debate. I joined because I was interested, curious.' I'm trying not to babble, and ridiculously, I can feel my knees quaking. 'I learned a lot, although mainly I learned that I didn't want to stay. My atheism was too entrenched.'

The Minotaur shakes its mighty head, 'Yet, those lyrics you kept quoting, "*Knowledge comes with death's release*". You would say, "Some things we're just not meant to know yet." Are these the words of an atheist?'

I nodded remembering those words from the Bowie song *Quicksand*, 'I know, but adolescence is a confusing time and faith, a confusing thing. I'd been in this confusing place of not knowing for a long time even by then.' I stop to breathe, having the music in my head calms me a little. I recall my sister asking me if I believed in G-d when I was six, sitting halfway up the stairs, like Christopher Robin.

I remembered the impact of growing up as a Jew had on me. When I was four my father was the president of Bristol's Orthodox Synagogue. I know this sounds impressive but this wasn't through any religious adherence on my father's part. It was just a natural progression, as he was simply an extremely easy-going and gregarious man, living in the heart of his community. Being a family of atheists and belonging to the Orthodox Synagogue was never an issue, for us anyway, as it was all about tradition. We adhered to some of the practices and felt Jewish, but belief was not relevant. My parents were brought up as Orthodox Jews and so we were brought up the same. But the experiences we brought home with us, with regards to the religion, were rarely positive ones.

'I remember how Dad would say how pleased he was that the prayers were in Hebrew, because he could speak it but not generally understand it. He would tell us of one morning prayer, said only by the men, as the women were not allowed to join in, which, when translated, basically thanked G-d for not making him a woman!'

'And this still troubles you?' Digging the knife in my Achilles heel.

'Yes, of course, the divide between men and women, the fact that women are considered unclean because of their life-giving monthly bleed is something I've always struggled with. We've created a hugely complex world. I can't just snap my fingers and make everything work for me in the world out there, just because I now believe in G-d in here.' I stop myself, mustn't lose my temper, we've only just started.

'Just checking.'

Is it mocking me? Do Minotaurs have a sense of humour, or sarcasm? Yet, as I said, it is me. I slip into reverie, recalling my years of attendance at Chedar, Jewish Sunday school (pronounced *chay-der* with the same gravelly throat sound the Spanish use to say the name Juan).

I give a big sigh.

It was here that I properly met my rabbi close up rather than from afar at the other end of the synagogue. Reverend Model was an old man, the archetypal rabbi with the grey beard, the kapel on his head and a sad look in his eyes. At some point it was explained to me that he and his wife had arrived here after the war and that his wife had lost most of her family in the concentration camps. I remember being told that they now resided in the house next to the synagogue and that she was basically a 'screaming wreck.' Years later I came to see that this experience, although far too young to understand at the time, shook any religious belief I might have been toying with.

I now believe we all come into life open, still very connected to spirit, but if this isn't developed we quickly lose it. I think that story affected me more than I realised. Having five planets in Pisces, this would have tweaked at all my feelings of empathy, causing me to shut any doors that might have remained ajar, and given any faith I might have developed a huge knocking.

I can see the old man now, on his feet, so frustrated. I can hear him shouting 'Sit down, boy!' with his thick German accent.

My Minotaur raises its head, it is listening to my thoughts.

His strong pronunciation just gives the Sunday school boys ammunition feeding their feelings of indifference towards him. They are just out of their private boarding school for the day and looking for any opportunity to play up. What do they care? His voice gets higher in pitch and with each order his authority slips away.

I can see that all he wants to do is teach the Torah; help these young people the way it helped him. However, the years have changed people's aspirations so much that what he believes to be a balm, to the next generation, just creates feelings of alienation.

'All I remember,' I say, 'are boys scrambling over the desks and shouting irrelevant and irreverent jibes. The poor reverend would slump into his seat exhausted and I would just feel totally distressed, helpless to do anything …' I feel the pressure build behind my eyes as it does each time I think of this. 'I know my heart bled, and still bleeds for this gentle man, lost in a world he no longer comprehended and that dealt him so much pain.'

'But you didn't heed his words, you didn't get what he was trying to teach you.' There is derision in its tone.

'No, you're right, I couldn't pretend I got it. I just paid attention in class, I couldn't bear to cause him any more pain. I became a "good girl" and so won the end of year prize each year.' I laughed, but the laughter soon dropped away.

Many years later a cousin of mine became head teacher of the Jewish college in this same private school. He told me when the parents of these disruptive boys came to discuss their children's problems with him, he knew that all they really needed was a hug. Maybe this is something we could apply to all of us. It took years for me to discover this was my story also.

*   *   *

At the age of fourteen my whole family reached a place where we no longer wanted to be a part of the synagogue. We became Jews by birth only, connected by our bloodline and no more. This unusual phenomenon, to be of a tribe, identified by its religion but yet able to denounce it, has long continued to fascinate me.

I have tried to imagine how this might have looked through

the centuries. Each age bringing changes in atmospheric pressure, from trauma and prejudice to peace and assimilation, like the bellows of the melodious but haunting sounds of a concertina breathing in and out over my ancestors' shoulders. My hope is to see a pattern emerging, a broader brush that might reveal the bigger picture of understanding here. However, the complexity of the Jewish mindset, its relationship with the other religions in the Abrahamic trinity, like the ructions of an estranged family, is possibly as unfathomable as it might seem.

The fact that I am here as a Jew means my family stuck it out and survived. That in itself is to be celebrated, yet carries its burden. But does discarding our ancestral wisdom, like a school leaver in a fit of pique, throwing away their textbooks, solve everything?

This is how it was for us, questioning everything and yet questioning nothing. We continued as a family, artistic, though typically academic and intellectually led. The word of G-d held no real meaning for me and the phrase 'hallowed be thy name' never entered my conscious mind as a serious idea. 'G-d' had been reduced to a swear word, not as an atheist's attack on G-d, just part of my thoughtlessness, part of my lack of engagement with my heart. 'Oh, G-d' frequently issued from my mouth and if I was ever reprimanded for doing so I would simply tell myself 'I didn't mean anything by it'.

As I internalised this overused response, one I would hear time and time again over the years in the battle against discrimination, I wondered if we would ever acknowledge the power of carelessly placed words.

Being prepared to give myself a break here for past transgressions, this aspect of living in my head, completely cut off from my body, was to frame the next twenty years of my life, unaware that part of me was still searching for something.

'Do you remember when you stopped going to the synagogue?' my Minotaur whispers in my ear.

I feel my shoulders tense again, a voice sharp as ice from the shadows, 'Very clearly,' I reply, 'as a family we, I, haven't been back there since.'

'And when did you join the Baptist Church's Young People's Fellowship?'

'The YPF?' I know where this is going, 'yes, also when I was fourteen.'

'And how long did it take to clock that one?' Its great head tilts towards me. 'You know, you were quite rude about their beliefs. What must they have thought, you, with your arrogance and cynicism?'

'They were generous towards me, they were generally good people.'

'You thought they were misguided.'

'At the time, yes. It's complex.' I felt we should leave it there.

I mused on the fact that whilst leaving the synagogue was a gradual thing, as an adolescent, I suddenly became aware that most of the friends I was hanging out with at the time were all becoming born-again Christians. The timing didn't match up until I looked back quite some years later.

Had I stopped to wonder why I joined, I think I would have said that from an intellectual, theological, and sadly, a deeply cynical viewpoint, I was simply fascinated. They invited me along to their Sunday night gatherings where I began to learn about a far more modern take on religious life. After fourteen years of learning about stories of the Old Testament and how to keep your home according to the rules of a Jewish G-d and tradition, here at the YPF, I didn't learn about the bible, I learned about how they lived day-to-day in a Christian way.

What they made of this young, mouthy, Jewish atheist in their midst I'll never know, other than they were very open-hearted towards me; unfortunately, I'm not sure I can say the same for myself.

I was interested but I was not touched. I would argue my atheist stance with my new friends as neither they, nor their G-d, met me in any way that changed the way I felt about the world as I saw it. Their G-d who art in heaven, as it had been in the Jewish teaching, was a distant man in a distant place that, I felt, just wanted to control me and judged me (although they would constantly refute this) when I strayed from the path. So I remained stuck in my head, disconnected from myself and everything around me.

At the age of seventeen I removed myself from the group having made some good friends and done some interesting things. In particular, as music was, by now, my thing, I remembered playing my saxophone in church as part of a religious, theatrical piece and I even learned robotic dance performing in shop windows, nightclubs and car showrooms.

Two years later I went on the traditional pilgrimage to Israel. My parents have never been but paid for each of us, myself and my two older sisters, to visit a Kibbutz. This was an amazing and life-enriching experience in so many ways, but a key moment for this story, was when the Kibbutz took our group of volunteers to the Holocaust Museum in Haifa.

We were a small group of volunteers at this Kibbutz, ten English, one French, one German and one Canadian and out of the few of us that went on the trip I was the only Jewish one amongst us.

We were given a tour around the whole museum but the only

thing I can remember of it now, was being shown a film of the opening of the camps at the end of the Second World War, the horrific footage of the piles of skeletal bodies being bulldozed around the site. Seeing this was not a new experience for me but as the film came to an end I heard sobbing coming from the other end of our line of seats. I see the Minotaur's shadow stir,

'Hmm,' it pipes up, 'the young German lad?'

'It was strange, we discovered that this was his first glimpse into his country's history. Such a harsh introduction, and what I took from that was a belief that Germany wasn't ready to face its truth.'

It still feels very fresh in my mind today. However, just recently, when retelling this story to a German friend and contemporary of mine, he absolutely refuted this idea. He told me that in the eighties Germany was falling over itself to educate its young about its past. When I looked at him with astonishment, he then added that maybe this wasn't the same in all parts of Germany. Truth, gleaned from a single incident, can be so easily misconstrued and show itself to be an extremely complicated and multilayered concept.

The Minotaur knows there's more and brings me back to the small group of Kibbutz volunteers as we comforted this young man as best we could. And I know there is nowhere to hide in its presence.

I remembered how all eyes then turned to me, and they asked, 'Why aren't you crying? You're Jewish!' I pause in thought.

'And what did you say?' It asks.

I take a deep breath. 'I said, "I've seen it all before."'

As a young Jew growing up in England there were many television programmes educating those who wanted to know about it. I'd seen enough already.

'Do you believe that to be true?' It cuts through my thoughts.

'That's what I said, because I had,' I affirm.

'You, who tell everyone you cry at adverts and soppy films no matter how many times you watch them?'

Yes, but I had also studied Brecht's *Threepenny Opera*, which portrays how humans can be desensitised to shocking experiences the more they are exposed to them.

I decide to leave this for now. I can sense the walls are still way too thick to penetrate.

I began to realise how I had buried this deep for thirty years and built a thick barrier between myself and this story. What would it take to shake the foundations of this wall and realise just how much I was kidding myself? At the tender age of nineteen, I was very much stuck in my head and able to brush all this aside with ease.

* * *

I love the fact that Jews do not write the word of G-d as it is considered too sacred. They have many ways of saying his name, but the most beautiful way, it was told to me recently, is that the original word for G-d, 'Jah-way' (written in Hebrew script as YHWH from which we get Jehovah), is actually the sound we make, the in- and exhalation, when we take our first and last breath. This is like the Om or Aum in Hinduism. Picking up these pearls, little pieces of wisdom, would bring my newly discovered spiritual understandings of the ancients, and my old Jewish story together. This would help me find my way home.

I can see the shadow of the Minotaur rubbing its nose in the earth and stamping its feet, not angrily just impatient to get on. So much to clear out.

Another year has passed and I am now a professional musician, 'don't you laugh!' I point a finger at the Minotaur as I hear it snort at this statement. I have a moment of feeling brave, but it doesn't last.

'Well, I was invited to join a pop band, to go on tour. Isn't that being a professional?' This was my passion and now my work. After training as a classical clarinettist throughout school and deciding I wasn't good enough for all that serious stuff, I finished my A levels, took up the saxophone, and got into the world of rock, pop and attempted some jazz.

The band was going to Hong Kong for three months and it all sounded very exciting and on the surface it was, until it all went pear-shaped almost as soon as we arrived. This is a story in itself but amongst all the mayhem we did encounter a very amazing woman, a guru, who took three members of the band under her wing.

We learned to meditate and listening to her talk of G-d I realised that this was not like the G-d I had heard about before. She talked about higher dimensions and about connecting to the core of the Earth. She spoke of physics and vibrations and all sorts of mathematical theorem that tied very beautifully into her spiritual ideas. She definitely opened something in me that I knew was longing to come out.

One of the first times we arrived at her stunning home she had set the room very beautifully with dim lighting and aromatic incense. She seemed very intuitive, almost psychic, but my initial cynicism reminded me of the time I had played in my Baptist Church at home and thought then how easy it was to influence people with theatrical sounds and lighting. I stayed with these thoughts as she asked us to meditate with her. As I sat cross-legged in front of her, my discomfort was highlighted by my bad posture and how out of alignment I was.

She explained that she believed that rather than thinking of G-d as above as 'in heaven' she understood that the core of the Earth held energy and great power. Since my awakening I have gained a whole understanding of this, learning to see Mother Earth as the reflection of the Creative Heaven, G-d energy, and this sits very comfortably with me now. Back in Hong Kong in 1986 it was just a little seed cracking open. She asked us to breathe, imagining that the Earth's energy was entering our body, through the soles of our feet, and rising up and out of our heads.

As I started to do this, although my mind stayed in its disconnected state, my spine started to feel very strange, like a metaphorical steel rod was being pushed slowly, but comfortably, up my spinal cord. She complimented me afterwards and although I was being asked to connect with my body, sadly, back then, my mind and physical body were not on speaking terms. I did, however, as I do with all things like this, log the call for future reference.

On the other side of the story, as far as our musical careers were concerned, things were slowly becoming untenable just being in Hong Kong. After six months of being completely ripped off, the band decided to cut its losses and found work as a covers band in Singapore to pay back our debts which had amounted to a tidy sum.

In Singapore the regime imposed on us by our employers was rather a shock after the laid-back lifestyle in Hong Kong, but we soldiered on with the long rehearsals and nightly performances. One day, during a rehearsal, we could hear something interfering with our music as it came through the speakers. We realised that the engineer in the control room was listening to something on his own personal system while he was mixing our music for us.

Our speakers were somehow picking it up. When we asked the engineer what we could hear, without knowing what we were letting ourselves in for, he offered to lend us the cassettes. They were tapes on, of all things, Satanism.

Like a flower that had been gently teased open in Hong Kong with the new knowledge we were gaining, the words of the American preacher on the cassettes were like a pair of secateurs; they weren't just closing the petals, but lopping the bud off completely. It was a brutal and rude awakening as the preacher, in his fight against Satan, turned his attack on Eastern spirituality. He not only castigated all that we had learned of this ancient wisdom but also our work as pop musicians. The recordings spoke of the devil using his powers to infiltrate and corrupt the minds of young people through meditation and modern music. He spoke of subliminal messaging in music that could turn young people away from G-d to Satan when he came to Earth. He explained how powerfully this can work by explaining how playing music with hidden messages in shopping malls has been hugely successful in reducing shoplifting. It felt like the finger was being pointed directly at us. They also had live exorcisms which, if they were real, were terrifying and if they were fake, were extremely distasteful.

I knew, even at the time, that everything he preached about in his over theatrical way, was coming from a place of fear and ignorance, especially where Eastern spirituality was concerned. But it was impossible not to be influenced by it.

I couldn't get away from the idea that if I chose to believe in a G-d then I had to believe in this devil I had just encountered too. With little hesitation I decided that I'd rather close the door on it all and sleep at night. I retreated to, what I believed was, the comfortable world of atheism.

I sense my beast is choosing to remain silent here. Being aware that at this tender age, I was clearly not ready to question my fear. I just feel relieved it doesn't want to probe me further on it right now.

Returning home to England, I continued my life as a musician and teacher, happy as can be expected for a cynical atheist living in a cynical world, totally in my head and not really aware that there was any other way to live. Faith was as far from my thoughts as it had ever been.

*　*　*

In time, I got used to the idea, with the everydayness of life, of abandoning my search for a greater truth. With this, somewhere deep within, I came to understand how I, we, as a society felt abandoned, lost. Millennia of trauma has encased our hearts in lead, as we build wall after wall around it to protect ourselves from feeling this pain. So, each new generation, a little more distant from its heart, hands down a slightly smaller version of love each time.

So what we are reduced to, as we remain living in the remote, outer regions of our hearts, is mirrored by our modern-day Minotaur. Although change is well overdue, and these walls more than ready to be brought down, sadly for the moment, our collective Minotaur will have to content itself being left shivering out in the cold. Each day, however, its shadow grows bigger and ever more powerful, as it feeds on our pain.

I am always wondering, while we are being pushed ever closer to the brink, what will encourage people to choose change, and whether it will require a degree of faith? I sense my Minotaur breathing a little more heavily. I brace myself. I have embarked on this inner journey to find answers. 'Ask and you shall receive', is a phrase I have come to feel comfortable with. As I settle myself into my breath and allow an empty space to open, the words flow in.

'Up until 500 years ago everyone would have had faith.' It speaks.

I nod slowly, not wanting to interrupt.

'But now you're living in the age of science and technology. You believe you live in a secular society.' I let it continue. 'And you have simply given G-d a different name, one that is no longer sacred, no longer hallowed. You are now looking at G-d through a smaller lens, calling it science, exchanging the telescope for the microscope.'

'Yes, you're right,' I interjected, 'in general people aren't interested in religion, spirituality or any form of divination like the I Ching or astrology, anymore. None of these powerful tools hold any weight these days.'

'Corruption and fear has censored them, bringing about the loss of all your ancient wisdom. The wise ones have been silenced, their words stripped of worth and reduced to facts and figures.' My Minotaur holds a confidence I cannot match.

'Yes, and anything we can't prove, we've just removed as irrelevant, like the bully who removes the games they don't understand from the playground. Nobody likes to look stupid. Yet, it's the parts we refuse to acknowledge that hold all the answers, the vast majority of the universe that we have simply swept under the carpet as unimportant.'

'Careful, you are stepping into dangerous territory, language you don't fully understand?'

'Yes, I know.' I decide it's time to retreat and ground myself before I continue again.

PART 2

In the summer of 2013 I arrived in Frome, moving with my new partner, Mark, into our new house, twenty-five years after my trip to the Far East.

The previous year had been magical and challenging all at once and it felt like quite an achievement to have got this far because the process of getting here had already demanded a huge amount of faith. I also knew there was still a way to go before we could relax.

Although I was fully aware that everyone around me seemed to be hugely stressed, I was thoroughly enjoying the process. I felt that this particular part of the journey was my personal story. Wrongly or rightly I saw myself holding the wand here and so I had to be completely confident all would end well. I just needed to convince everyone who was travelling with me to remember to breathe; frequently they forgot.

Realising that although I hadn't travelled far to reach this moment in my life – only about 20 miles – I had certainly journeyed a distance in my heart. This new place that I inhabited was a place that held the concept of faith at its core, something that my younger self would have felt quite uncomfortable with. However, it still had its challenges.

The town, although situated at the far eastern side of Somerset, felt like it could be in France; the part we lived in at least. Our house was positioned at the top of a hill called Catherine Hill with its famous, though newly installed, cobbled streets, independent shops and numerous coffee bars. We'd walk pass beautiful Georgian architecture as we descended into town and gradually, with each step, the buildings would age, becoming more higgledy-piggledy, back to the mediaeval times. Passing countless plaques of people of interest who had resided there and historical points of dissent, we soon realised this wasn't a town that has remained quiet through the ages. With the famous Cley Hill for a backdrop, it practically shimmered with vibrancy. Those that felt this vibration were being drawn like magnets. Every time Mark and I arrived home, we'd look at each other and say, 'we live here!' with an almost childlike excitement.

What I was aware of, was that Frome hadn't always been like this, previous decades would have found it a cider-drinking, fighting town. I had played a gig here twenty years ago at the Frome Festival but that was in a field somewhere outside the town. Over the years I began hearing whispers of things changing for the better but never experienced it myself until now.

It might also be important to acknowledge that the term 'better' is very much a subjective viewpoint and there are those who really dislike what has happened to the town; its gentrification. It was only four years later that the expression, 'Make Frome shit again' adopted from our neighbouring city 'Make Bristol shit again' came into being. A concept in constant need of scrutiny.

I sat for a moment with these paradoxes, the many that pervade our lives continually, and that we continue to ignore to our detriment. Working hard to ensure my lens kept expanding as I believed I saw society's contract, I wondered, how did we arrive at this point as a race?

I feel my Minotaur's shadow creep into sight. I try to imagine its face, too horrible to look at, but my curiosity is strong. Again, I feel my ribcage tighten and my throat too.

'Are you asking?'

'I suppose so, yes, but,' I pause. It looks at me to continue. 'I have an idea of my own.'

'Go on then.' Its voice is booming and I feel like I'm back at school. It's not a good feeling.

I try to compose myself. How to tell this cultural story without sounding stupid, arrogant, smug or just needing to get off my high horse wasn't going to be easy. Reminding myself of all the things I've been accused of through my life, and probably rightly so, isn't something that makes me feel comfortable but neither is holding a faith in a secular society. Some of those labels I may have given myself, but over time I've certainly come to realise that fitting in just becomes less important.

'I see it as a story, a journey.'

'Nothing new there.'

I suddenly lose my nerve. 'Maybe I'll start with one of my own first.'

* * *

I had spent most of my life in Bristol but about eight years previous to this arrival in Frome, my then, long-term partner, Andy and I moved to a village just outside the city. This was a place of extreme beauty, rural and picturesque; a huge change for me.

It was here that the phrase, 'we live here!' was coined and repeated over and over. (I felt very blessed to be able to hold onto that.) Here our sixteen-year relationship began to break down and by 2010 I found myself alone in my little village. It had been a heartbreaking and painful split but through it all we were determined to remain amicable and in this we were successful.

By the end of 2011 Andy, now my ex, had moved back into the house which still belonged to the both of us and we were living, I felt, as brother and sister. Within weeks I was introduced to

Mark, currently residing in Wiltshire, by a mutual friend, and it wasn't long before we both realised that this was serious.

Initially it was proposed that Mark would buy Andy out of the house, as we believed this was the only financial option available to us.

However, I think it would be safe to say that Andy wasn't at all happy with this whole idea and by the summer, he managed to find a way of buying me out. He thought this would upset me but actually, apart from the finer details of making this work, I was overjoyed.

Andy's new partner, Stella, had exactly the amount that she needed to buy me out once she had sold her London flat; the synchronicity gave me the feeling there was divine providence at work.

As Mark and I met often in Frome, because of its perfect geographical proximity to where we both lived, we started appreciating how much there was on offer, for a small town anyway. When we began to discuss where we wanted to live together there were a few towns to choose from but the more we thought about it the more obvious it became. There really was only one place that simply felt right.

In January of 2013, on our first anniversary, Mark and I booked a weekend in the hotel in Frome where we first met and started house-hunting. By the end of the weekend we had found our new house.

With Stella's flat and our own house all going through the normal proceedings everything seemed like it was going to be plain sailing. How wrong we were. Days before everything was due to be completed, Stella's sale fell over. We were all devastated.

That same day I was due in Glastonbury for the launch of an anthology. It is a collection of inspired essays, stories and poems, called *Secrets and Signs of the Glastonbury Zodiac* and I was very excited to have a story included in the volume. Before the evening event all the authors were invited for a special ceremony at a house once owned by the woman who rediscovered the zodiac a century ago, Katharine Maltwood.

I arrived at the meeting point, knowing I was late. I saw the last car drive away and realised I had missed my chance of attending the ceremony. Only the day before everything had seemed so perfect, now I fell into the Magdalene Chapel feeling utterly miserable.

As you enter, from the High Street, there is a small finger labyrinth before you step into the gardens and chapel. I traced my finger around it slowly and purposefully. Once inside the tiny chapel, I offered a prayer to Mary Magdalene, someone with whom I have gained a deeper relationship over the years. I slumped into a chair and asked for her help with our small housing crisis, even though I sensed little could be done in the short term. I was soon begging with tears falling down my cheeks. There were only one or two other visitors but I didn't care who was watching.

The next day we began picking up the pieces and working out how we could move forward. Obviously everyone was disappointed, the estate agents, vendor, buyer and of course the four of us.

That afternoon the phone rang and Mark went onto the doorstep to answer it as the reception was poor in this, not so remote, village.

After some time he came back in the house.

'I'm not sure, but I think something amazing has happened,' he said.

'What's going on?' I had no idea who he had been talking to.

'That was the estate agent. It appears Frome is offering us a lifeline.' He went on to explain that there was something new that certain estate agents were experimenting with and Frome was leading on. Basically it was risky but, once we had exchanged, it allowed us an extension on the completion date. However, it also required us to pay rent until we completed, to cover our vendor's second mortgage. As long as Stella's flat went through in time all would be well. This was where the deep breathing was needed, but I was completely confident that I was still working under universal law, especially as my prayer to Mary Magdalene had been answered so swiftly.

We agreed, signed on the many dotted lines, for this was a complicated affair, and moved in. Stella's flat then went back on the market. She was under a huge amount of stress and I assured Mark I would shoulder the debt with him should we lose our deposit. However, I was absolutely convinced it would never come to that, still holding onto my faith.

I remember people saying to Mark, 'It must be very worrying for you, having put yourself in such a precarious financial position.'

I would butt in with a, 'No. it's not at all worrying, it's all fine.' Infuriating I know, but I had to hold my course. Keeping my 'forward' memory positive was an imperative. What is in the past, cannot be changed, it is fixed; what is in the future is filled with possibility. With the heavens already proving to move mountains to get me into my new house I was not going to give in to doubt and fear now.

So here we were, living in the picturesque town of Frome. A mediaeval town that was bigger than Bath in its day. It has a history of revolution and like its neighbouring city, Bristol, has a personality outside the run-of-the-mill. This perfectly suited where Mark and I were at, as individuals and as a couple.

Towards the end of November, as the dark nights were closing in, Stella's second sale date was in sight as was our deal. Suddenly there was a wobble challenging my rocksteady conviction once more.

Some while before this, I had formed a back-up plan. At the time, I had absolutely no intention of using it as I knew I wouldn't need it, such was my certainty. I had found myself talking to various friends, who were of a certain age, and becoming aware that many of them had retired with funds in the bank doing very little. I remember casually mentioning, to one person in particular, the idea that I might need to borrow a considerable sum. I asked if he would be interested in doing a deal, offering far more than the current low interest rates. He was very happy to oblige. With this in the back of my mind I stayed calm.

Suddenly, here we were again. On the first Friday of December, which I named Black Friday, Stella came through with the terrible news that her buyer had definitely pulled out. We were stunned, our deadline was getting too close for comfort and we were in danger of losing the house and our deposit.

Hours later, we were visiting Mark's mum in Surrey who was suffering from a long-term degenerative disease. The telephone rang once again, but this time the call was to say that Mark's father had passed away. It was a huge shock.

Staying only for a cup of tea, we got back on the motorway to visit Mark's stepmum and his father's body, then returned home to spend the next two days holed up in our house just being quiet. These two days became my own personal retreat, challenging my trust and faith in my new life, with my new partner, in my new house and my new town.

All I could do was pray. I prayed to G-d, to anyone who I

thought might listen and I also prayed to Mark's father. When I felt I had gathered enough positive energy within myself I sat at my computer to compose an email. It was an honest account of my position, moving into a request for a loan with a good rate of interest offered, but making it quite clear that if this was not within their means they should feel no problem with saying no. I picked six friends to start with. They were people that were not connected to Mark as I truly felt this was my mess to sort out.

I pressed send and with it put every ounce of my positivity. Also playing out in my mind, was the fact that my father wouldn't have approved of this kind of dealing with money. But, I knew that this was exactly what I was hoping to look straight in the eye; the fear of money, or rather, the lack of it.

The first response was a very apologetic 'no', but that was fine as it showed me that I was not upsetting anyone with my request. The second was a 'yes'. This was from the same person I had initially proposed the idea to, and I had my first 10,000 pounds. The trouble was I had quite a few of these to bring in.

I had cast my net close to home to start with and I had my second list of people to ask ready if needs be. Well, who was I kidding, I was probably going to need a third or even fourth list. The problem was, did I have that many friends with money I would feel comfortable asking? I could hear my Minotaur whisper in my ear, 'Unlikely', but I closed my ears to it, knowing I had to stay positive.

Within a day or so, Mark, who was fully aware of what I was doing, mentioned some new friends we'd recently made in Frome.

'Did you send your email to them?' he asked.

'Of course not!' I was quick to answer as I thought I'd made it really clear that I did not want to involve Mark in this, so was not asking any friends we had made together.

'Well,' he looked at me disbelieving, 'I did tell them of our situation, but not in a way that was leading to any requests for money.'

'Yes, and …'

'They've just written to me offering us two-thirds of what we need.'

This was a vast sum of money and I was left feeling speechless. Once again, my prayer had been answered. However corny that sounds, that was exactly how it felt to us. The rest was kind of plain sailing. My parents and Mark's stepfather helped us out with the remainder and with my first offer, we had our target. In fact, we had to turn one offer down. It felt unbelievable and all the deals were negotiated within a week. We were all jubilant.

My father was incredulous, exclaiming that we'd invented a new type of banking, but I think peer lending wasn't really a new thing, just new to us.

There was, however, a grey cloud hanging over all of this. Mark's dad's funeral was a simple affair and I felt honoured, as a newcomer to the family, to be asked to play. This felt like a fitting way for me to offer my thanks from any help from upstairs.

Once all this was dealt with and everything in place, Stella's flat sale went through the third time without a hitch and within a few months all debts were paid. Some were a little reluctantly received as the bank was no match for the interest rates we had been paying. It was champagne all round and the four of us celebrated the end of an arduous journey. We had survived, unscathed and happy in the end.

* * *

'You must have put your parents under a lot of strain during those few months.' It was a weighted comment and I knew my Minotaur wouldn't let me fudge the issue here.

'Yes, I can't deny it. But my dad always taught me, by example, to take things as they come and not let them get a hold of you. My G-d, he said the war was the best time of his life.'

'But you didn't speak to him about your finances during those few tense months?'

'No,' I had to admit it, 'but the thing was, they weren't tense for me, that was my whole point. I was just walking towards my goal, which I could see clearly in front of me.'

'You just ignored all the obstacles.'

'Yes, I suppose I did.' I closed my eyes in thought. 'I kept asking everyone to see the positive, that while everything was moving forward, the only blocks were the ones we put in our own way.'

'Still it must have been a worry, and for Mark and his family too.' It was insistent.

'Yes,' I could sense my irritation rising, 'but, there was no point in worrying while nothing had actually gone wrong. It's like, what's the expression, praying for what you don't want. I refused to adopt that mindset.'

All I hear are the echoes of silence.

*   *   *

At last I was free to bring my attention to my new home town. There was so much going on in Frome it was difficult to choose where to put my energy first. During the months before we moved in we attended many events which would give us a taste of the town we had chosen for our home. The first event was

Frome's Festival of Ideas where we heard Satish Kumar speak about how living in a town was the best sized community to engage in. Having moved from a city to a small village, my next move to a town felt like something out of a fairy tale; Goldilocks and the Three Bears comes to mind.

The first group I joined was the Frome Friends of Palestine. It couldn't have been made simpler for me. The first meeting that I could attend was across the road from my house. The room was full of strangers, apart from one person I had met a few years back, but I was warmly welcomed.

First on the agenda was their contribution for the Frome Festival which just happened to be a music event. I knew that you can't just waltz into a town and a demand a good slot in a festival. So I listened as they finalised the details then asked politely if they needed a support act. They were delighted. The main band, *Seize the Day*, has been fully engaged in activism for years, and I had already encountered their amazing performances at Glastonbury Festival. This wouldn't be the last time I'd come across them.

Each meeting of Frome Friends of Palestine (FFoP) became a learning zone for me to gain a greater understanding of what was going on there. This was something I had previously turned rather a blind eye to. Couple this with the fact that, although my parents were deeply distressed by the actions of the Israeli government, they certainly held a biased viewpoint, just like many British Jews. For me, a 'head in the sand attitude' had just seemed easier. This wasn't helped by the fact that I had mostly stopped listening to much of the news some years back as I felt it wasn't helping me find my way through life with joy.

'That sounds very shallow.' My Minotaur's voice is always to the point.

I would have to get used to the idea that it was never far away.

'You're probably right, but I have never held the media in high esteem.' Was I leading myself up a dangerous path here?

'Don't you find people criticise you for this?'

'Of course, and probably rightly, but I have never believed that what the papers say holds a great deal of truth. So I'd prefer to be uninformed rather than making myself miserable being ill-informed.' But I'm digressing.

I explained to my shadowy companion how the group is widely known and respected; that it works to raise awareness, help those in need and do what is important to bring about change and fairness to a society that is deeply divided. With all my work with the Golden City this was hugely important to me. I saw the Golden City, as not only representing our heart, but also representing Jerusalem, the spiritual heart of the world. It is a microcosm, a conflict that mirrors the conflict within us all.

I needed to resolve this and joining the FFoP felt important and symbolic. I hoped to join with an open heart and an open mind. Although I thought I was not under any illusion about the Israeli government's actions over its dealing with Palestine, I certainly wasn't prepared for the onslaught of information that was about to be thrown at me. I was going to have to find a way to reconcile this with myself.

'Did it rattle your cage, shake the foundations of your faith?'

I smile. 'Of course not, in fact the opposite.'

My faith had become the glue that held my resolve to work through these painful truths. It had not let me down before and just because the road was getting rockier, this was not a reason to look for an alternative route, on the contrary, just a requirement for sturdier boots.

* * *

Holding faith in the core of my being has enabled me to trust that I am being looked after, that I am constantly being guided. When the coincidences pile in, even when the reasons aren't obvious in the moment, time and patience has taught me to relax into the flow and see how all is eventually revealed.

Even though I was fully immersing myself in my new community I was still being called back to Bristol frequently.

One such time I was invited to play my harp at a Peace One Day event at the Bristol City Hall, a day full of speakers, storytellers and musicians.

Among them was Michael Eavis, a farmer, though not your average one. When asked to talk on this subject, he exclaimed, 'Well, I don't think I know much about peace.' However, having kept the Glastonbury Festival ploughing ahead for the last forty years or so, he went on to say, 'But, I certainly know about conflict.' He astounded me with his light-hearted approach to the fact that conflict was not something he was scared of. Whenever he found himself in a difficult situation he would eagerly rub his hands together, claiming he thought of it as 'fun'. I was in awe; conflict for me was something I always feared.

However, as we reached the last session of the day, the MC introduced a woman who he said was the most amazing woman he had ever come across. I listened with curiosity but also a level of scepticism.

Her name was Jo Berry and she had lost her father, a Conservative MP, in the Brighton bombing in 1984. Ever since, she has worked to find peace with this huge loss. In 2000 when the convicted man was released after the Good Friday Agreement, she was adamant she wanted to meet him. Her strong desire for peace enabled her to let go of her need for judgement which in turn forced the man to stop trying to justify his actions. Her conviction was such that he had to face his own position for the first time in a new light. He would say afterwards she gave him no choice but to open his heart.

Working together ever since with reconciliation, travelling all round the world, I was deeply moved by her sincerity and the tireless motivation that drives her work to this day. At the end of her talk she casually mentioned that she now lived in Frome. I simply laughed to myself, of course, where else? I found myself quickly falling in love with this quirky town and its active community, for all its problems and divisions.

*   *   *

Faith is often considered by those who have none, and I would include my younger self here, as something outdated, that no longer has a place in our modern world and that those with faith are often considered delusional. This has led me to become an onlooker in society; taking an outsider's perspective.

It saddens me that the idea of choosing to live by the heart rather than the head should bring up such mistrust and conflict between people. The belief that something like this is either right or wrong, good or bad could, I feel, be taking us down a very dangerous road, into the mouth of the Minotaur itself.

I shudder at the idea.

'Not at all advisable,' it growls at me, aware of my every thought, but its sudden appearance no longer makes me jump.

'I know,' I say, 'it's time to grow up, and sift through the shit for the treasure hidden below.' I take a long look at this shadow of a beast in my midst and steel myself. What is so frightening, once you get used to it? 'You know the more I see of you, the less scary you seem.' I smile a little.

'You're saying you're growing accustomed to my face?'

'That's what they say, though I still can't see your actual face, just a silhouette. We are expert at getting used to things, even when they're not good for us, like the analogy of the toad sitting in the pot of water on the stove. It just gets used to the increasing temperature until it boils to death.'

'What do you think we're doing that's so terrible?'

'We've lost sight of the truth, the peril we've put ourselves in. As our lens gets smaller and smaller, we lose sight of the bigger picture.'

'What's wrong with that, that's how we get to the heart of things, real truths?'

'Do you really think so?' I'm not so sure.

'You must be careful not to fall into the trap of judgement yourself, the one you're so hooked on catching others out on.'

I feel the beast's reprimand, and it's not wrong.

It continues, 'The idea that the toad would jump right out if it was put straight into boiling water, sensing the danger, only tells half the story. Do you think if the toad leapt out, if we changed things now that would solve all our problems?'

'Are you telling me it's all in the timing. That we're just not ready yet?'

'Maybe? What do you think?' It's giving nothing away.

'I know we're kidding ourselves if we think we've got it all sussed. If G-d is everything, the universe itself, when you take out the heart, soul, purpose and story then you're left with science, but it's still G-d. It's just a smaller slice. Every time we think we're there, take a closer look down the microscope, someone goes and opens a door to a whole new realm.'

'Careful.'

Haven't we been here before? OK, deep breath.

'But the quantum world is so much more than a load of formulae, not something you can understand with just the head. I really think it's time we started holding up our hands and say, "OK, we give in, there must be a higher wisdom at work here."'

'I understand that you're worried that we're only looking at the physical world, forgetting to see things as relational, but this bigger picture you talk about, how wide is your telescope set?'

I feel immediately defensive, 'Big enough that I can see we have our creature comforts but we pay for it by losing everything else.'

'Everything? Don't start getting irrational, not at this early stage.'

My hackles rise, 'We've become irrational! Ridiculous even. How else could we destroy nature, stripping it bare so that we can hide in our cities, separate ourselves from the wonder of the stars with our constant electrical lighting, our ability to truly appreciate the moment as we fill every second with constant noise and distraction.'

'You done?'

'No!' This isn't me, I really don't know where this is coming from? 'We have more stuff, but more debt, more medicine, but no less death or illness. We have lost our sense of community and even our sense of family. As we've become increasingly isolated, our mental health as a society is in crisis.'

'But you're not answering my question.' It is pushing me now. 'Are you hoping to bring everyone back to G-d?'

I stop. 'Oh G-d,' I revert back to type, 'is that what it sounds like I'm trying to do?'

'Well, yes and no.'

'You know I'm not.' I'm not sounding sure. 'The thing is, I don't believe we've lost our faith, it's just now we have faith in the economy, in prescription drugs, faith that everything is improving, that the plane is going to stay in the air when it takes off.'

'Yes, and that has a solid base for many people.'

'But I don't believe it's enough. When I was looking, the G-d I found only mirrored the limitations of my expectation and understanding; the small lens. I always believed there was something more, and that's why I found it eventually.'

'But you still called yourself an atheist,' always cutting to the chase.

'Yes, and I probably never was. The seed that was sewn in me in Hong Kong, when I look back now, just showed me I wasn't ready to find my faith. So it remained dormant for when I was.'

'Exactly,' it leaps in. 'And thirty years later, you can see the seed in society is not dormant, the delicate saplings are growing and you have to be careful not to trample on them with your impatience. Timing is everything.' Its tone was sobering.

The words land but I'm not done. 'I suppose I'll never understand those that believe there is nothing beyond human intelligence and science.' I reply in resignation.

'You need to understand if you want to understand the world better.'

'Well, if I am deluded, if that is all there is then all I can say is "G-d help us!"' I laugh at myself and close my eyes.

I have to acknowledge that there are many paths and I am just one of many travellers here. The journey we are all on has its own timing and has to take its own natural course. Some will arrive at the destination with the help of G-d, some without. I just have to be careful not to fall into the trap of being judgemental.

I believe that faith holds a key and it is my hope that it's a door you have already opened, or have at least considered opening. For me, it's a gateway to letting go of wanting to be in control, of needing to know all the answers, attributes of the human ego, that have brought us to this breaking point. We have so much work to do and yet we would do well to do nothing; a wonderful paradox. It is my hope that faith might guide us towards a greater wisdom and that this might make things OK, even more than OK.

I know that love is key, and faith the driving force that turns it.

CHAPTER TWO

THE SECOND PETAL: SURRENDER

Thy kingdom come. Thy will be done.

The Cicada

I live, I die.
I fall so I might fly.
My flames rise high,
Like a rose from a thorn, like a rose from a thorn.

I came to rest a while, after the longest mile,
Left behind by the tide while all else was swept aside.
Your branches sheltered me, do you remember me?
Though tired and torn, I bring the dawn.

As the sun casts its light upon the evening sky
My shadow magnifies me
Though I am small my shadow knows eternity
I am all things, I am nothing, I am free.
I am all things, I am nothing, I am free.

I am an offering, myself to you I bring.
Like a flower on the tallest bough.
My heart may feel the sting but my soul shall always sing.
I am reborn, I am reborn.

As the sun casts its light upon the evening sky
My shadow magnifies me
Though I am small my shadow knows eternity
I am all things, I am nothing, I am free.
I am all things, I am nothing, I am free.

PART 1

It's time to move on to the next petal, just a step away. I had reached a place of peace with my faith, and although it wasn't my intention to quote astronauts through this enquiry, I remember it was Armstrong who said, 'One small step for man, one giant leap for mankind.' I think I like the idea that from the astronaut's viewpoint they get to see the bigger picture, one I always feel helps to gain a better understanding of where we are and where we might wish to go.

The second petal is the petal of Surrender, *Thy kingdom come. Thy will be done.*

This is a truly powerful and utterly beautiful concept. One that, when grasped fully, surrendering ourselves to the greater forces at hand, enables us to find ourselves at the perfect place at the perfect time. I'm sure you, like all travelling on this path, have experienced a taste of life when everything suddenly seems an effortless flow of grace.

Is this something our culture has lost? I sense the idea of surrendering has become a difficult concept for many. To most it is seen as something negative, rather than the positive intent it requires. Nowadays, to surrender means to yield, to give way and is generally experienced on a battlefield by the 'loser'. The concept of winning and losing soon turns into one of judgement.

The need to win is part of our insistence that we are the good guys and therefore, in the right. Like a spiral works its way up, tightening our coiled spring of need, the belief in 'us' and 'them' heightens into the idea that we are the best and there can be no one better, no one more intelligent than ourselves.

This is upheld by our left brain mindset – and although I know that our brains do not work in this simplistic left/right mode, I am using this term metaphorically to keep my ideas clearer – isolating ourselves from each other in so many ways. As we create the idea that we are alone in the universe then we have to be the top of the chain. We have built this into our scientific insights, as we have rewritten Darwin's findings, putting 'survival of the fittest' at the top of his list rather than 'love' as he did.

Resistance is the issue here and we are living in an age of complete resistance to many things. Even the revolution that took us into the age of mechanisation, over the last few centuries, is all fuelled by power based on resistance and friction. It's the role of the ego to resist while the spirit yearns to surrender, I find it interesting that we are now beginning to look at energy that is living and free-flowing. This paradox that lies at the heart of our existence means that it often takes extreme conditions for people to reach that ability to let go and recognise how amazing it is when you do. Yet, aren't we now living in a time of extreme conditions?

With all this fundamental to our cultural and religious beliefs, how could we begin to take on the idea of surrendering to something we don't even believe exists, especially when the G-d we have come to know is, for some, something quite grotesque. In many ways, our society believes we have engaged in this battle and won. G-d is dead and surrendering is farthest from our thoughts.

I have to acknowledge that my hopes for any change in our society is dictated by my own ego. I pray my Minotaur will help me let go of that need.

Personally, letting go should be something I do well. It is the Piscean trait built into my make-up. Pisces being the last month of the cycle, like the Russian dolls analogy, holds all the others within its universal oceanic waters. This, I believe, is an invitation to expand my vision and view our journey as the Mayans do. They are the time keepers and understand heavenly cycles better than most, mapping up to seventeen cycles of different heavenly bodies at play. They know about the long game and have prophesied a return journey; the end of the great cycle.

I had reached a place where I could see that cycles gave a truer view of the world than the linear time we have come to invest our energy in. The smaller our cultural horizons the more I felt the need to expand mine. The Galactic Year, or Great Year as it is also called, is made up of twelve galactic months. Each is an age of approximately 2,000 years, the time it takes for us to travel through each sign of the zodiac. We are currently at the end of our time in Pisces and are entering Aquarius. This holds great portent, like a time of renewal, a rebirth, the like of which we've not seen in 26,000 years. It is my hope this shift in time and space will be so powerful and so beautiful we will be able to do nothing but surrender to its will.

I mused on the idea that first I had to know I had something to let go of. How can we know what we don't know? It took thirty-two years of living in my head, thirty-two years without comprehending the nature of resistance or what I was resisting before I could surrender to the will of G-d. Being human is an amazing thing, when you finally sense what obstacles we have put in our own way to stop ourselves learning pure love and real happiness, you do have to laugh; otherwise the grief can be overwhelming.

* * *

Now, I am ready to drop fully into this petal, into the memories that flow into my mind. They roll in and out like waves on a sandy shore, some tease my toes but when I forget to pay attention, some capsize me, tipping me over and drenching me in emotions I thought I'd left behind.

The Minotaur is hovering but only on the edge of my awareness. It's waiting for me to roll the dice of judgement, one false move and it'll pounce. But I am ready for it, no, I'm hoping it will step in.

I am brought back to my time in Bristol, England, at the tender age of twenty-one after working in the Far East. I was in no mind to surrender to G d's, or anybody's will. I started to build my career as a musician and music teacher, happy in the knowledge that life carried on whether I was searching for something more or not. A kind of cynical stoicism pervaded my life and I surrendered to the idea that, as the Bowie lyrics stated, I might have to wait for death to find the answers I was looking for.

At twenty-five something happened which changed my life but it would take me decades to fully understand all the significant cards that were playing my hand.

I sense my Minotaur lift its great head, turning its ear slightly, and I am conscious that I am feeling even more at ease with this.

'Come on in,' I call out. 'No need to hover in the shadows, I know you want to hear.'

It doesn't move.

'It's my grandma, you see, she had had a fall the year before and the cancer in her body just took hold.' I pause to think about this. 'Sadly, at the time I didn't really see it as having that much of an effect on me.' I check how this lands.

'Is that a bad thing?' It's not giving anything away.

'I suppose it is what it is, but I was wrong about it not having an effect on me. I was just too immersed in it to see. It took me twenty years to fathom out what impact it did have, but at the time I didn't feel deeply upset. I just didn't feel that close to her.'

It says nothing and I am left with my jumbled up memories.

'I remember when my sister took her English O Level early. She was fifteen so I was eleven. When she told Grandma that she got a B, she just went silent. Then after a while she said "now an A is better than a B, isn't it?"' I laugh ironically. 'I've never forgotten it.'

For years I held my heavy heart, wondering where was that typical, lavish, doting affection that I believed most Jewish grandchildren receive, no matter what the result? Over time, it felt like it was stamped on my DNA, always destined to be a B student, even though the comment wasn't even aimed at me.

'Did you always take on everybody else's pain but your own?'

I mentally ducked. Was that a criticism? But more importantly was it true?

Grandma was the only grandparent I had known, she was my mother's mother and although she was an exceptional woman, she and my mother had a difficult relationship. I've heard others use the expression more of a smother than a mother. I knew, sadly, my mother wouldn't disagree. The paradox was that everyone who knew my grandma, knew her to be a wonderful, broad-minded, intelligent woman but for anyone who was a direct descendant nothing was ever good enough.

'That was your belief,' it pointed out. Another blow, I'd have to be quick to dodge all these. I recalled how a few years later when my sister had been dating a black man for two years, realising this was serious, Grandma decided she didn't want to see him anymore. The 'not in my backyard' was very clear yet considering she'd visited South Africa and sat in seats designated for black people only, it was a confusing message. My sister, thankfully, didn't give up and two years later Grandma got over herself, having not seen my sister for all that time, but it was a tricky moment in our family. I remember one moment when Grandma was more upset that Dad had called her a 'stupid woman' rather than about what she had done.

But now, in 1991, she was gone and it was the end of an era for the whole family and particularly my mother. However, when we returned from the funeral my mum spoke about how she and her brother and sister had sat down and discussed their feelings for the first time. They each expressed similar stories of how they felt towards their mother and my mother particularly felt that her siblings were the favourite and that she therefore, felt unloved.

To me this was untenable. If they all had said the opposite, that they all felt that they were the special one, even though I don't like favouritism, that would have seemed so much better, but no, Grandma was suddenly being revealed to me as a woman unable to show love to any of her children. How could this be? The conversation sat on my chest like a huge weight.

My mum, sensing time as the great healer, felt far more fondness for her mother as the years fell away. I am ashamed to say that I continued to judge her terribly, on behalf of my mum, of course, though it remained buried deep. Unaware of what I was holding on to, I only felt its effect, the tightening and breathlessness in my chest; what I would later understand to be a feeling like a gasp of unexpressed grief.

'Soon after the funeral, I got two chest infections. It never felt bad enough to go to the doctors, but ...'

'But?' I imagine it mirroring my 'don't make a fuss' face that I don't even realise I'm making.

I shrug. 'Well, I was lucky as this was the forerunner that soon turned into asthma. Many die from similar experiences.'

I can tell it thinks I'm being overdramatic and I sense my defensive stance stepping in.

'It was only my breathing technique as a saxophonist that helped me through it.' I pause, 'Well, maybe there was some extra help?'

It looks at me quizzically.

I continue before it has a chance to comment, 'It was quite scary. I was going round in circles, fighting to force the air out of my lungs, but then I would just breathe in another huge lungful of air in my panic. I didn't really have a clue what was happening but then I sensed, I was being given an image in my mind, like a diagram from a textbook, to explain what was going on to help me relax.'

'And it worked?'

'Yes, it took nearly an hour but I got my breathing under control in the end. This continued every night for nearly a week. And then it came back a month or so later and I went through the same process all over again.' I reiterated, 'I was very lucky.'

'Do you believe you were being helped?'

Easy for me to admit it now but at the time I don't know what I would have answered.

It soon became apparent that my grandmother, being the amazing, self-made business woman that she was, had left a considerable sum to her children. My parents were comfortably well-off and of a contented nature, and my older sisters were already on the property ladder. It was agreed that I would be the recipient of this early inheritance, on the condition that I bought a house with it. It was an amazing gift and just before my twenty-sixth birthday I moved into my lovely home.

I felt very lucky but I also felt weighed down by feelings of responsibility and guilt. This is multilayered and something I believe our Western religions have burdened us with. So it only took a few months before I was waking up one morning and just turning over in bed made me feel out of breath. I rang the doctor and was officially diagnosed with asthma.

At this time I didn't connect any of the dots. I'd suffered from eczema as a child and had been prescribed with steroid drugs to treat it. I knew this suppressed it rather than curing it so was not surprised when it popped up years later as its cousin, asthma. But I didn't wonder why this would happen at this stage in my life. This would take another decade or two, as I hadn't started to consider factors such as cause and effect or synchronicity yet.

* * *

Life was settling down for me and after I'd lived in my house for nearly a year, I was beginning to enjoy the novel idea of 'staying in', a new feeling of contentment. Although I had met Andy a few years back, something suddenly clicked, we started dating and fell in love. This was the beginning of my first long-term relationship.

However, by the time I was twenty-nine years old, though enjoying my career as a musician and teacher I was already wondering if there was any more to life than what I could see in front of me. Something inside me knew there was but I was becoming a little less upbeat, a little less confident and slower to laughter. But I had a good life, fortunate in many ways but also a little lost. It didn't matter how many times I told myself about seeing the positives in my achievements, I couldn't seem to work out what happened to the bright hopes I had as a young adult.

I can see myself pouring over a syllabus, contemplating doing the degree I never did after my A Levels, wondering if I can make up for lost time.

I am aware of my Minotaur scrutinising my face, 'Was it that bad?'

I try to make light of it, but my face is speaking volumes, 'I knew my playing brought joy to people's lives and I helped loads of people realise their dreams of being a saxophonist, but ...'

'But, what?'

'I wasn't Mike Brecker.'

'You know what, most people don't even know who that is.' It almost chuckles.

'No, I know. But at twenty-five I set myself a Stalin like five-year plan to become a great jazz saxophonist and by thirty I had to swallow the bitter pill of knowing I had failed. But I tell myself it's OK.'

'But it's not, is it?' It stops for a moment, 'Is it OK that Brecker, this incredible musician, dies of a brain tumour in 2007?' Suddenly life feels harsh.

I take a deep breath. A degree, what a ridiculous idea, I hated organised education as much as I hated organised religion. What was I still searching for?

*   *   *

While this is happening, myself, Andy and a good friend, Seb, were all members of a big, party band and Seb's own band too. The three of us hung out together quite a lot at this time. Then Seb began to show signs of cracking. I had seen her try to pull herself back from the brink of an emotional breakdown before but this was bigger than any she had encountered previously and sadly Andy and I were right in the firing line of it all. Like an explosion we were flung afar and could only watch from a distance as Seb fell into the depths of her psyche.

Two years later, we heard she had found her way back up to the surface again. When another year passed, I thought it was too late to attempt to retrieve the friendship. It was Andy, in the end, who felt that perhaps it was time to reconnect. He was always far more intuitive than I ever was. I went along with it and we all arranged to meet. In the end we met her separately which was to be for the best.

I turned up on her doorstep, one foggy November evening of 1998 hoping that we could rekindle our friendship but expecting nothing more. I arrived at nine o'clock at night, a little apprehensive. Her flat had not changed much and we were soon back to our old way of being together. The healing process started as she revealed her experiences over the last three years, moving back in time, till we arrived at the point of the breakdown. We crossed the pain barrier, picking through the debris of where she and our friendship fell apart and began reconciling it all.

Then she brought me back to the present day and started talking about the universe and her new place within it. She talked about love and light and the energy beings she was connecting with and as she spoke she began to radiate such an amazing energy I could not help but be deeply moved.

She was talking about G-d, but not in any way I had heard

about before. In fact, it had really nothing to do with the words she spoke, although I knew that my left brain was enjoying the information it was being fed, but my body was feeling things it had never felt before. It was hugely overwhelming, so strong I was being drawn to tears, not tears of sadness but tears of joy and release. I was coming home for the first time and I felt the doors of my heart open.

All that searching was over, even though I didn't realise I had been searching till now. For the first time I could see that G-d had nothing to do with a person, nothing to do with words, orders or rules and regulations; G-d was just the vibration of pure love. It took hold of you, wrapped you up and dissolved into you beyond all understanding.

The more I surrendered the more I could let go of all the smallness of my existence; the fear, the pain, anxiety and neediness.

I remember sitting in her flat, she had never been your run-of-the-mill kind of person and now the flat seemed all the more out of this world, although there was nothing I could put my finger on. Her striking feminine beauty contrasting with her intense masculine energy created a fascinating dynamic. She pulled no punches.

'We will be given a choice,' she said, 'we will have to choose between the shadow and the light,' I thought I understood but I realised I only got a fraction of what she meant. At the time I saw it like a day of reckoning but actually I soon realised it would be a daily, a moment by moment, occurrence.

This surrender was like a remembrance, so different from anything I had encountered before. This time there were no disappointments because there was no one to disappoint me; no teacher, no guru, no preacher. Just the two of us, trying to work it out together; trying to find ways of keeping connected to the love.

We spent a great deal of time together over the next year, Seb using me as a sounding board to bounce all her experiences off, and me, like a sponge, soaking up all the energy she was emitting. Often I felt the tears roll down my face, while I was laughing at the same time.

As we stepped into the new millennium, my old friend had transformed herself into something quite new. It soon became apparent that she needed to spread her wings. She sold all her belongings and ran away to the City of Angels to be an angel in Los Angeles and find her spiritual home. For the next six months I felt quite abandoned. Even after a year with Seb, I was still stuck in my head and I desperately needed guidance.

Andy was on his own journey, giving up so many things, eventually drinking nothing but hot water, but I needed something more than a physical transformation.

Thankfully I was soon brought in from the cold by another fellow musician who had also had an epiphany. I joined a crystal healing group and started meditating daily. I threw open all the doors onto this new path and within months this new deep practice healed my asthma.

*   *   *

'So that's it, end of story, you've found what you were looking for.' My Minotaur is teasing me.

I imagined looking straight into its eyes. 'What's that book called? *After The Ecstasy, The Laundry.*'

'This is the problem when you have no tradition of wisdom in your culture, you don't realise that this is just the first step. This is where people get lost.'

'You mean like the people who start believing they're the

new Messiah.' I guess it knows I'm teasing.

'They've been touched by this powerful energy and find there's no one to guide them through it. For those who don't recognise what's going on, it can seem like a madness.'

'They're not crazy, I get it.' I am keen it knows I understand.

'Yes, and for a society that is lost, and reaching its own state of insanity, whilst still thinking it's on track, anyone who steps outside the agreement of the group will evoke feelings of discomfort.'

'Like the toad in the boiling pot, we're steadily adjusting to the madness. We're terrified of breakdowns, just like with Seb, we were all trying to pull her back from the brink. But breakdowns can be the key to a breakthrough.'

Its voice is resigned but resolute, 'Yes, I am the face of that void; the face that few are prepared to look at.' A flicker flashes across its shadow.

I catch a glimpse, prompting me to seize an opportunity, to probe further. 'Our scientists are going through the same experience, well, some of them anyway.'

'Oh yes?'

'I've watched so many documentaries, learning how, over the centuries, they've searched for answers by dividing and separating the world, until they even split the atom. When Einstein opened a door into a world beyond comprehension, the quantum physics took us from the very small out the other end where everything exponentially expanded until it reconnected into oneness again.

'I have so loved watching scientists wriggle and squirm as they are forced to surrender to what Einstein unearthed. This discovery was so ahead of its time, even he struggled to believe it was possible. Now a century later, though it still seems like a madness to many, I believe there is no choice but to see the complexity and simplicity of the quantum world.'

'Yet we still resist.'

'Yet we do,' I agree. 'I have heard scientists since talk on television about having self-confessed nervous breakdowns as they struggle to go against all their logical ways of working. I sense that when you're dealing with higher dimensions, third dimensional logic as we know it, couldn't possibly continue to work in this new realm.'

'Just like time, logic is a creation of our limited mindset. And you mustn't forget the importance of timing here. The scientists are playing their part making sense of the world in their words and that is vital for the coming together of this journey. This new frontier, that we have only peeked at, works beyond the limits we have placed on our world but we can only arrive there when we are truly ready.'

'I hear you.' I recognise how my impatience is constantly tripping me.

When the time it right, I believe the universe will open us up to understanding and feeling with our hearts. This is clearly a difficult concept for those who only use their heads. But when we make that quantum leap then quantum mechanics will begin to make sense. We have to choose to surrender to it first. By letting go we will begin to release ourselves from much of the pain that we experience in modern life.

When we fully embrace this, our hearts will guide us back to a state of connection, and as more people get it so the whole of the human race will. It's the hundredth monkey theory[2] and that's a theory that stands up even in our scientific world.

*   *   *

I could see this beast, who seemed softer to me each time we met, wasn't ready to end the conversation.

'You speak of "remembering" like we've been here before.'

It's not letting me get away with anything. I pause to think. 'Well, you know I see things in images and patterns. I'm building a theory but possibly lack the diligence to substantiate it.'

'That sounds dangerous,' it says and I feel the severity in its voice.

'But we all have roles, don't we? Mine is the visual one and I hand it to others to add the detail. It comes from a different place but doesn't make it wrong?' I am keen for reassurance.

'Go on.'

'I see it starting in the Garden of Eden,' I begin tentatively, 'a world steeped in spirituality where we are in G-d and G-d is in us; G-d being the garden, life and everything.'

'But of course,' it interjects, 'that wasn't the beginning. You're aware that back then the cyclical nature of the world was understood, rather than today's linear view. But sadly the cyclical cataclysms that we experienced washed away most of the evidence of the world before this. It also removed much of the understanding and wisdom.'

I start to relax, a little relieved, 'This understanding is important to me here because it ties in with my desire to reconcile my inner conflict between my religious understanding and my spiritual one. I know they have come from the same place, like brothers, I believe, one makes choices that serves it, and the other does not.'

'Yes, that is a truth, a story.'

I continue, though watching my step, 'I feel that when we left the Garden of Eden, we believed that we were thrown out for a wrongdoing. Immediately we brought down the judge's hammer on ourselves creating feelings of abandonment and separation from our home, our hearts.'

'Another story, and if it rings true for you and helps you navigate these difficult waters then that's fine.' Its clarity is fierce.

It does and it will. I bring my thoughts to the idea that like any child that feels abandoned by its parent, the child always blames themselves, feeling guilt and self-hate. This belief was immediately passed down as hard-working Cain couldn't handle Abel's feelings of contentment, just hanging out. His anger gets the better of him, resulting in Cain killing Abel; the first story of blood spilling that we are told.

This sets the backdrop for future generations and we have been living with this trauma ever since, creating a shadow over our lives.

'Do you agree?' I call out.

It doesn't answer me directly but poses another question, 'At the heart of all this, deep in our troubled psyche, you believe there is a desire to return to the garden, to G-d?'

I feel there is a paradox between our negative relationship to G-d and my belief that we never left. It's just what we have constructed in our minds. This is the story that has taken us down this shadowy road bringing us to this pivotal place.

'My understanding, as I came to see it, was that Abraham created a new religion out of this story, that saw G-d as separate from himself and that Judaism was the first of the three Abrahamic religions that still stand today.'

I saw how we kept moving away from pure unconditional love into our heads. Sadly, the lessons that have remained in my memory from my Jewish education, more than any others, are the judgemental ones. I remember that the Jewish G-d is a jealous one and that women are subordinate to men. This immediately separates ourselves internally, putting us in conflict with our head and our heart – our masculine and feminine attributes; our Cain and Abel – and prevents us from surrendering to love and wholeness.

'And there we see it again, the next family split with Abraham's sons, Isaac and Ismail, as Ismail is forced to leave the family, and a new religion is born out of his journey.'

'And where are you going with this?' It is probing me now.

'My need for reconciliation and surrender has always drawn me to the story of Christ. He offered us a chance of union as he tried to bring us back to love. But again we denied his truth, sacrificing his life and built a religion based on Peter's.

'Sadly, yet unsurprisingly, all I see after this is more conflict. In the 1100s this trilogy of religions sparked the Holy Wars, a beautiful paradox, as we began to kill each other in the name of G-d, in the Holy Land. Then, as our view of G-d contracts and the judgements we attribute to G-d expands, we continue the journey into separation in earnest. Hundreds of years of witch burnings and all our connection to the Earth and our emotional wisdom is lost. The conflict between masculine and feminine rages as the heart is finally conquered and our head becomes the ruler. The heart "surrenders" into the Age of Enlightenment.' I can't stifle my feelings of horror and I know I have to pause.

'It is a horror story indeed. But remember the world started its journey out of the Dark Ages at this stage,' it helpfully points out.

'But I struggle to see the next stage of our journey as light.' I muse on the thought that this was also the Age of Discovery, when Europeans set out and 'discovered' new land, staked their claim and systematically began ethnic cleansing those who already lived there.

I'm getting distracted. I move on. 'My problem is that all

I can see is an inability to resolve any kind of conflict.' In the West, this led to religion continually splitting apart into its many denominations, weakening, until it lost its power to the monarchy. The kings of Europe, with their need for supremacy birthed an age of Imperialism, which, led by their flagship, the USA, reached a climax in the twentieth century. Here we had collective conflict manifesting two world wars with death tolls and collective trauma growing exponentially. It feels shocking.

'I can see why many thought G-d had completely left the building or if not, had a major part in smashing it to pieces. No wonder this led to atheism becoming a norm.' I stop and sigh.

'Don't forget this is a journey and only when the lesson has been fully learned can we return.' Once more my Minotaur is trying to bring me back to my heart.

'But meanwhile this journey is an internal one of disconnection that is bringing us to the brink of our own destruction.'

'If that's what it takes,' it replies.

Although this sounds terrifying, when we surrender to its necessity we will realise that the journey into separation has also brought us many important gifts. The development of science, quantum mechanics, the Internet and space travel being just a few. All of these breakthroughs have given us the necessary tools to understand who and where we are so we can reorientate ourselves as we journey home through our dark night of the soul.

Then, almost as a whisper I hear, 'Have you forgotten Lilith?' And my Minotaur retreats to the shadows.

PART 2

In the small market town of Frome, things were beginning to move a little faster and the need to surrender to anything was far from my thoughts. I had only been here a year but I already felt that things were taking off. Being such a sociable community I had already met many people that I felt comfortable calling my friends and I was buzzing from events to meetings and gigs on what seemed like a relentless current of engagements.

The surrounding countryside meant that walks were easy to find and plentiful, and although I missed my garden, Mother Nature wasn't far away and really I didn't have the time to tend a plot of my own; better to leave her to her own devices. Life felt full and abundant.

By the summer of 2014, I had performed at the Frome Friends of Palestine's Frome Festival gig, supporting Seize the Day, this amazing group of musicians, their songs dedicated to activism, once more, stirring my soul.

As a regular member of the FFoP by now, I had attended many talks and meetings, filling my head with stories of resistance, pain and injustice. Before I had time to take it all in, the news came that Gaza was under fire from the Israelis. The onslaught of suffering galvanised the FFoP to set up a stall on the high street in Frome, collecting signatures for our MP, hoping to give the Palestinians a voice.

We met many interesting people on the streets during those campaigns. Four hundred people signed our petition, which filled us with hope. However, we also encountered some strong opposition. Now, of course, you would expect this, but sometimes I was caught off guard. One fearful, German, Jewish couple warned us that we would soon all be killed by the Islamic extremists, one by one. Another passer-by felt too strongly to sign the petition and when I probed further he mumbled something to the effect that he wished Hitler had finished the job properly the first time. In hindsight I was glad I couldn't find the words to respond.

There were many rallies going on in London but eventually there was a call to make the next one the biggest that summer. As the day approached, I decided to join a few of the others from our group and we booked our coach tickets to London. The Saturday in August arrived and we boarded the bus. It was the first demonstration I had been on since the biting temperatures of the anti-war march in February 2003.

Thankfully, this time it was a warm summer's day and although we were a small gathering, maybe 30,000, it felt powerful and determined. I sensed a note of anger in the chanting and explained my discomfort to one of the members of my group, who said to me,

'These people want to win at any cost. They're not interested in peace.'

I looked at him with obvious disappointment, but felt no desire to judge. I quietly stood firm, not sure why I had come, but feeling my presence there was important to me and that was enough.

We headed up one of the main streets towards Hyde Park and came to a standstill. This was not unusual but as I stood on the edge of the wide snake of people, watching the shoppers on the pavement watching us, I became aware of a hand reaching out to me. The hand took hold of my arm and gently pulled me towards him. I looked at the hand and up to the man's face and I found myself standing in front of an elderly, dark-skinned man with a kind smile. In a wonderfully rich accent he said to me,

'I presume you are Jewish?'

'Yes,' I replied. He simply looked back at me and kept repeating, 'Thank you, thank you,' over again.

I just said, 'It's what I have to do.'

He told me that he was Egyptian and how he had come to this country thirty years ago. He only gave a piece of his story but what I felt was just how overwhelmed he was by my presence here and I was completely overwhelmed by his gratitude. Although this encounter only lasted minutes by the end I think we both had tears in our eyes. We gave each other a farewell hug as the march started to move once more and I now knew why I had come. It was beautifully simple, my true reason for being there had been recognised and that's all I needed.

*　*　*

At the next meeting I was introduced to a Christian woman who was interested in interfaith. We met several times over a cup of coffee. We talked about the Church and our differences, but we also had much in common and she offered to lend me a DVD called *Two Sided Story*. This was a documentary following a reconciliation conference in Israel where thirty Israelis and Palestinians met to find a way to peace by working together, processing and understanding each other's trauma.

The documentary was tough, beautiful and fascinating. Watching the facilitators work with the group, to enable the participants rise above their beliefs of 'I am right and you are wrong' on both sides felt transformational. It was so inspiring to see how empathy could replace hate when stories and tears were shared. It filled me with hope and with her and the film maker's consent, we put on a public viewing.

As the summer continued, the FFoP put on a talk by Ilan Pappe, an eminent Israeli historian. He had found it increasingly difficult to continue living in Israel, following the publication of books such as *The Ethnic Cleansing of Palestine*, so he left. He became a professor at Exeter University.

He had spoken in Frome before and been well received but we weren't sure how many people might turn up this time. We knew we had expanded our mailing list with these 400 signatures so we decided to hire the Cheese and Grain which is the town's biggest venue, hoping we hadn't overreached ourselves. We were also nervous because the only evening available was a Tuesday night after the roller disco at eight o'clock.

From 7.30 pm onwards people started crowding into the bar. At 7.50 pm we tried to hasten the children from the main room as they casually finished their drinks and took off their skates. Grabbing everyone we could for the quick change act, after we scrambled to set up a bookstall, a food stall and 350 chairs, the room was buzzing.

No one was left wanting, the speaker was clear-sighted, eloquent, without rising to anger or blame. He explained how the Israeli government are open to allowing people to see what most governments keep top secret regarding their internal affairs so he was able to reveal much about the psyche and the exploits of the government. He didn't use notes and didn't bombard us with statistics. Whether you agreed with him or not, this man gave a fascinating talk.

We were prepared for opposition: how could you not be with such a controversial speaker in such controversial times? Actually, when it came to it, we were slightly disappointed that the speaker was only preaching to the converted here in Frome. However, we were not quite prepared for what did happen.

Soon after the talk began we were aware of some music playing. The main doors opened and in walked a man, dressed as a prisoner from a Second World War concentration camp, complete with a yellow star sewn on. He was playing the theme from the film *Schindler's List* very beautifully on the clarinet. Immediately four men from our group, as arranged for such an occurrence, got off their seats and approached the musician. It wasn't a bad protest, in fact it was very musical, but it was, after all, interrupting our speaker whom all these people had come to hear. If we had wanted to hear music we would have come on a different night.

As he was being ushered out, he called out some words of protest against the speaker and at that point I realised I knew him vaguely. As a fellow musician and especially as Frome is such a small town, I felt I needed to talk with this man. The six of us left the room so that the speaker could continue.

Out of the room he said,

'Has he forgotten all those that died in the war, the six million Jews?'

I tried to reassure him,

'Don't you realise that the speaker himself is Jewish, as are plenty of people in that room, including myself. I understand how you feel but I assure you if you came in and listened you'd realise he has not forgotten our people who ...' I was indicating him as I spoke.

'I'm not Jewish,' he said.

I was astounded. His whole demeanour and defensive attitude came across as if he was a Jew.

I had to rethink. I didn't know what to make of this man anymore. I changed tack.

'Why don't you come in?' I suggested. 'You know you might

learn some interesting facts about what Mr Pappe is actually saying, rather than what you think he's saying.'

Unfortunately, he declined and remained outside playing his sad but poignant melody, adding what I believed to be a subtly fitting, though ironic, background to the talk.

* * *

What followed was a whole stream of letters in the local paper. My new Frome Jewish friends and I were now joined together by this ongoing discussion, wanting to understand what this all meant for us in our community.

We discovered the clarinet player was a fervent Zionist and a member of the Labour party. A new understanding of Zionism was beginning to creep into my awareness. Although he seemed to be coming from a caring point of view the messaging was mixed. No longer was this just about giving the Jews a homeland from a position of altruism towards the Jews but also a subconscious desire to 'send them home'. I felt somewhat embarrassed. How could I have been so slow to recognise the complex issues here.

While I was trying to unravel this, I learned that Hitler had also considered this idea. Now the media and party politics are still playing their part to create havoc between our religious faiths broadening the cracks between communities in this country.

However, I could see this was multilayered and I was falling into the trap of judgement once more. I realised I was only just skimming the surface, so I tried to suspend my emotions and immerse myself in the immense personal ocean of discovery I was on, surrendering to its complexity.

*   *   *

The petal of Surrender is possibly one of the most important parts of my journey. Personally, it is my greatest wish that I, like all those who take their first taste of champagne and want everyone to love it, succeed in opening people's hearts to join me in taking this plunge. The person who has had a piece of heaven, in the first stages of their awakening cannot imagine how anyone would not want this too. This is where evangelism is born, as we step from the awakened heart chakra and begin our journey through the higher chakras. The first we encounter is the throat chakra and we want to tell, no shout, our new truth to the world.

This would be my big lesson to learn, I knew I had a great deal of growing up to do, so I could move beyond the naive eagerness of the early phase of my spiritual journey and become a seasoned traveller; a guide not a tourist.

When you have jumped from the dizzy heights of the penthouse mentality of the individualistic ego and plummeted into the deep waters of the humbling energy of the soul, you know there is no turning back, and why would you want to? But it is important to be aware of the pitfalls on the way. Sadly our culture, so ignorant of this significant, limitless journey, has no maps – unless you are prepared to dig deep to uncover the wisdom of the mystics not readily accessible to the person on the street – to prepare or help us navigate our way and so many initiates get stranded and often abandoned in their first stage of development.

If you are only curious about your spiritual journey, then you may remain hovering near the edge for a lifetime. If you are filled with uncertainty then it can become like a black hole, impossible to avoid. However, because of the journey's all-encompassing nature, the ego will try to resist on every level.

Who can honestly say that when faced with a precipice we know we want to jump off, we can just do it? However strong the desire to fulfil our mission, and even though we know it will not just 'be fine', but actually be glorious, the fear factor is still strong in us. Not only that, the ego that clings to maintaining the small version of ourselves is constantly worrying about being dissolved; like the child who fears becoming the adult, the human returning to spirit. It is all down to fear of failure and that great human trait: self-sabotage.

How we long to plunge into that pool, the waters of freedom, that allow us to embrace all that we are meant to be. But to do that we have to cut ties with our personal angst, address all those issues that we are so bound up with, face our fears and let go of the safety of avoidance.

I have never been one to jump into anything. I always got into the swimming pool slowly, step by step, as a child. I forced myself to dive into a beautiful swimming pool, having never done any diving before, in a luxury pool on the banks of Mombasa when I was thirty. It took half an hour of standing on the side, shouting at myself inwardly, asking 'What's the worst that can happen? A belly flop, water up my nose?' I did it eventually but my goodness I took some coercing.

The issue with life is that there are many pools, and many oceans to jump into, surrendering all you have for the greater release of your small self so you can dissolve even further into a greater sense of who you are.

The next pool I had in front of me this time, seemed deeper, yet far more all-consuming than any previous I had encountered. My first experience with Seb had been so easy, like the painless bursting of a bubble, a beautiful release, I just jumped in. In retrospect, I knew I was being eased in gently.

When I healed my asthma, again that was easy, just a little discipline required to step into a practice, deepening my connections to my higher self. I could walk into this pond and do my lengths without complaints, in fact I loved my meditation time.

But asthma had come and gone a few times since and I had begun to see its ebb and flow in my life like an inconvenient, but necessary, visitor. Now I was reaching my own pain barrier as conflicts, embedded in my ancestral line, were beginning to stir deep within me. I would have to reconcile them if I was to continue moving forward.

These waters were so dark they were only visible to my subconscious, while my ego continued to hold onto the pretensions that there was simply nothing to see here. Even if I could have seen them, as the waters began to lap at my feet, my ego was far too busy looking up, trying to see what my next goal was, to see what was at the end of my toe.

This arrogant blindness that I was suffering from was an amazing lesson in itself. I truly felt I had done so much of the work; I'd investigated my life history, done a huge amount of healing, stepping from my head to my heart, and now I was simply keeping the mirror clean.

I hear a snort from the shadows. I think it was a stifled laugh.

'OK, OK, I also know that a sense of humour is certainly necessary here.'

'And of course, I'm laughing with you, not at you,' it replies.

'Why, thank you! But seriously, I understand the concept of exponentially opening doors, once you open one, ten more appear.'

'Yet, you thought you had it covered?'

I really did, I really thought I had done the "big work". That was, of course, the paradox; healing, like infinity is not a destination point.

I wasn't ready to take this any further, already feeling on dangerous territory. I sidestepped, some might say from the frying pan into the fire.

'Do you think our scientists will ever remember that?'

'Careful.' It was quick to respond.

As ever I was putting my mouth in gear before my brain, discussing science from the dangerous stance of an unscientific mindset. 'Don't get me wrong I am continually amazed and very excited how fast our scientists are reaching the same understanding the ancients had of our universe, but in an up-to-date language this time. But they do need to remember they are dealing with infinity, alongside a third dimensional view.'

'And how does that relate to what the ancients said?'

'That we are spirit beings living in a physical body, surely ...' I stop, I remember it's testing me.

'You don't think the scientists know much more than our ancestors?'

I start tip-toeing but I refuse to turn back. 'No, I believe this is a cyclic journey and we have forgotten so much. We need to reach in to rediscover the wisdom we've lost. The scientists can only get so far unless they surrender to what lies beyond the third dimension. This is the journey back to G-d, I mean what I call G-d.'

'Do you really think scientists are going to make this leap?'

I forget my apprehension, 'I not only think they will, I know some are already doing this. They are seeing the phenomena that occur there first hand. It's passing the insights back to the person on the street that will be the thing.'

'So how are you going to do that?'

'Uh, no. I'm not falling into that trap!'

One thing I have learnt is that we each have our own way of getting there, or not. All I can do is talk about my experience. My journey back to G-d was complicated enough.

* * *

It is important to note that I am, of course, using my own version of the word, but know that each individual has to find the one that they can feel comfortable with. I was very uncomfortable using the word 'G-d' for years, because of the diminished and corrupted view of G-d that I held. For years I tried using other words; 'source', 'oneness' the list is endless but all of them are simply running away from the pain that the word has brought into our world, through its misuse. The only way around this is to look it in the eye and heal the pain. I needed to use it and be happy with it, even if it meant pushing people's buttons, well, maybe especially if it did. When I finally realised what the word truly conveyed to me, my discomfort fell away.

'And how did others feel when you spoke of G-d,' it asked in a completely straight ahead manner.

'Of course it's hard, you lose people quickly, on many levels.' I reflect on this with some sadness. 'But how could I say I was coming home to G-d if I couldn't look through all the faces we've given him and confront him full-on? We each have our own issues and when we fear confronting them, our inner demons, or rather, you just keep growing in stature.'

My eyes instinctively look in the direction of the Minotaur and I wonder if its shadow hasn't shrunk a little?

I continue, 'I had a friend, some years back, whose flat was adorned with Hindu gods and goddesses. Krishna was his life focus. I remember discussing the issues he had with his strict Christian parents.'

– I reflected on the idea that while my feelings towards the Christian Church remain unchanged, I have been developing a relationship with the teachings of Jesus Christ over the years. As I learned about the differences between the teachings of Christ and modern Christianity, from my standpoint outside the Church, I could see how they have brought such pain; creating splits between families and communities –

I continued. 'I questioned my friend whether he hadn't just replaced Christ with Krishna so he wouldn't have to confront his own family differences.'

'What did he say?' My Minotaur was baiting me, I could tell.

'It's not important, what is important is that it was showing me what I was still ignoring in my life. It would be five years before I'd join the FFoP and start questioning my own distancing from my religious heritage.'

As I felt the Minotaur retreat I caught a flicker of light before it completely disappeared from view.

*   *   *

In my mind I see an image of the whole of humanity by the water's edge, contemplating the desire to jump in. Some have already jumped. Some are clinging to the sides knowing they should but are too scared, some are dipping their toes in, some are jostling for their place on or off the diving board and others are running a mile.

It is the role of the ego to cling to all we have held on to for so long, believing it is our salvation. The refusal to let go prevents us from stepping beyond the ego and embracing the limitlessness of our higher selves. Should we choose this then we might discover that drowning in the love that is a constant in our universe, is a blessing, not something to fear. It is also important to remember that it is our ego that hides this understanding from us.

This is not something the ego can discover by itself. People will either jump when the pain gets too much or be pushed by something beyond their control. As I hold to the hundredth monkey theory, I await the day when there are enough of us in the water to turn the tide naturally and we will all choose to surrender. The other probability is that the tide is going to simply rise to meet us.

If we enter the labyrinth with our minds in the driving seat we will be completely limited by our egos. If we let go of that, surrender into our whole sense of self, and step into the energy of our hearts we open ourselves to the wisdom of the universe, the connected nature of all things. Here we can be open to receive our highest truth, the answers that most serve us in that moment.

I considered what it would be like, as I gazed at the huge shadow not so far away, if you arrive at the heart of the labyrinth in fear. 'I suppose the idea of being devoured by you would seem like the most terrifying thing.'

'Am I not scary enough for you anymore?' It responds to my musing.

I wonder if my answer might hurt its feelings? Amazed at myself that this concerns me, I suppress the emotion and continue my train of thought, 'If you arrive there with an open heart then I'm thinking the Minotaur might bring an aspect of death into your life which brings the birth of something amazing, something beyond your wildest dreams.'

'Which is the greater illusion, death or me?'

I'm not sure I'm ready to answer this as yet.

Surrender, is about letting go, not fearing the dark. It's about falling into it so completely we can learn to navigate it once more and learn the lessons that can only be found there. Nowadays, I sense the dark is where we feel we have no control so we hate winter and run away to the sun if we have the finances. We are scared of the night so we put light everywhere and do all we can to avoid its profound depths. In a society where knowledge is king we are terrified of being seen not to know. Yet in the darkness there is gold. When we let go of the need to control, and let thy will be done, we find amazing answers, great leaps of awareness.

When we turn our back on the darkness, judging it to be evil, the Minotaur looms ever larger. I believe, black holes are the key to so much of our understanding of the universe, of ourselves, the magic. If we fail to look there, at the dark matter and dark energy, we are missing 96 per cent of the universe. In the silence of the darkness the mystery reveals itself to us. If we are too scared to go there we will never nurture ourselves, find the qualities we need to get through our dark night of the soul. In fact we've become too scared to even let ourselves enter.

The shadows flutter a little near me. 'I'm here, ready and waiting?'

I am startled out of my stream of thoughts. 'I know, and I know that our indigenous communities have known about this time for millennia, patiently waiting for us to choose to make that step into the unknown.'

'What will it take?'

I feel the tears begin to well up behind my eyes. 'Maybe that tide is coming, if we won't make the choice by ourselves.'

'Is that so terrible?' It's pressing me.

'I know, it's only our collective misunderstanding of death that makes us fear what is to come. I feel it's time to stop judging what we don't understand.'

'And that's what's got us into this state.'

'Yes, but I do not believe our time here is judged, judgement has come from humanity, not the other way around.'

I had learned how the apple of knowledge was the journey into our ego mind and the serpent the guardian of the ancient wisdom we lost. The serpent is the kundalini energy that rises through our chakras. This universal creative energy can be dangerous to the uninitiated, whose eyes are not open and are ignorant of the power of this wisdom. The ego construct that learns only about the outside world rather than the inner can be a danger to itself. As the relationship between the heart and mind becomes disconnected we are learning the hard way that the mind makes a good servant but a poor master.

Behind all this is Lilith, Adam's first wife, who, it is said, was condemned for claiming that she was Adam's equal. We are not taught this story, just as we are not taught of the black goddess. As the bible heralds the beginning of the white patriarchy so the story is rewritten with Lilith as the serpent. Then, slowly over time, like the Greeks with the Medusa, the serpent is stripped of its significance, as the symbol of sacred wisdom and fertility, and comes to represent evil.

'This seems to explain it all, why we are living in this state of forgetfulness, not knowing who we really are,' I muse.

'Indeed, like Osiris who was dis-membered before Isis patiently collected all his limbs and put him together again so he could re-member who he was.' My Minotaur's voice is more gentle now.

'Yes, so we haven't forgotten all the stories, have we? But we remember too many that teach us shame.'

'A damaging emotion that strengthens me.' It is softening.

'Exactly,' I exclaim. 'I don't believe that we should teach our children to feel guilty for having chosen the apple of knowledge, to feel guilty for enjoying sex or to think of G-d as someone who is watching our every move and deciding whether we are worthy of his love or happiness.' I pause for breath. 'No wonder our churches are emptying and atheism is growing by the day.'

I reflect on how much spin there is against any kind of faith or higher presence nowadays.

The belief that this only brings conflict and misery in our society, is understandably strong, Sadly, this has led to a greater sense of isolation, keeping each person an island, strengthening people's resolve to keep hold of any personal sovereignty with all their might.

However, I am the eternal optimist, and there is a growing desire for change and more discussion than ever nowadays When I heard that in 2014 the most googled question in London, after 'how to kiss' was 'how to meditate', my heart sang.

Not for the first time in my life, I found myself in a place that felt like a fast-moving conveyer belt. It felt chaotic, but thankfully, there was much joy as well. I was gathering people into my world that were willing to work with me, whether it was a passing, open-hearted Egyptian or some fellow, Frome Jewish women or some powerful peace-makers. The more I surrendered to it all, the more I realised I was no longer travelling alone.

CHAPTER THREE

THE THIRD PETAL: SERVICE

On Earth as it is in Heaven

Sulha (Reconciliation)

Take a seat at my table,
Though there's blood on our hands, we're like Cain and Abel.
We'll break bread, not our mothers' hearts.
Are we living by the grave or by the cradle?

Sulha, sulha, take a drink with me.
Sulha, sulha, a cup of coffee.
Sulha, sulha, take a drink with me.
Sulha, sulha, a cup or three?

How should we take our tea?
With a drop of remorse and a lump in our throat.
How should we take our coffee?
We'll keep the dream afloat till we believe in:

Sulha, sulha, take a drink with me.
Sulha, sulha, a cup of coffee.
Sulha, sulha, take a drink with me
Sulha, sulha, a cup or three?

And be free of all the rage and all the fear.
And be free, take some time to shed a tear.
And the pain will dissolve like sugar.

Sulha, sulha, take a drink with me.
Sulha, sulha, a cup of coffee.
Sulha, sulha, take a drink with me
Sulha, sulha, a cup or three?

We're tying ourselves up in knots inside
We can't eat, we can't sleep, we're like suicide.
We're banging our heads up against the wall,
Just remove one brick and watch it fall,
It's our call, one and all, for:

Sulha, sulha, take a drink with me.
Sulha, sulha, a cup of coffee.
Sulha, sulha, take a drink with me
Sulha, sulha, a cup or three? A cup of three?

PART 1

The third petal is the petal of Service. *On Earth as it is in Heaven.* I had already investigated this concept of 'as above, so below'. My first book dealt with service as an aspect of Virgo. However, there are many other faces to the Virgo archetype. Stepping into this petal would enable me to delve a little deeper into this particular characteristic.

The bridge between Heaven and Earth are symbolised by the Jewish Star of David. The two triangles, one pointing up, the other down, placed on top of each other represents the two worlds, the upper, higher dimension, and the lower, third dimension mirroring each other.

Maybe I was being reeled back in. I had come across it more recently, as a light-body, a three, rather than two, dimensional structure, like two pyramids intertwined. When visualised in meditation, it creates an energy field for raising your vibration; the Merkabah.

I begin to recognise how huge this is; the question of why we are here, and what our role is in life. I began considering our relationship to work and why this has become yet another soulless and arduous aspect of our modern lives. I realised we could greatly change this relationship if the idea of bringing Heaven to Earth became synonymous with your purpose, a life in service. 'Service' would take on a completely different objective, no longer meaning 'work' like we think of it today. I note how only just over a hundred years ago the Victorians had many people employed 'in service' which was not much different to what we would call slavery today. Those employed were expected to be grateful. Sadly, although we may have reduced this kind of occupation, slavery is still very prevalent in our culture; it's just more hidden.

I sense my mind is already going round in circles and after being in the stillness of surrender I now felt the need to get up and step into the feeling of doing as this petal implies, on the surface at least. As I emerge from my meditation and feel the movement in my body, the blood pulsing into my muscles, I rejoice in the shift in energy this brings. I notice new sounds, the birds conversing overhead and the insects busying themselves all around me. A robin, in a flash of colour and a rustle of air, enters my vision and settles on the ground near me. Its intent is finding food for its young. It pecks in the earth, a jab here and a jab there and pulls out a juicy worm. The elasticity of the worm is almost comical as it resists then springs out of the soil into the robin's face. Before the robin flies off, it flashes a look in my direction and I know exactly what it wants to tell me.

I see this beautifully simple life that comes into being with its soul purpose, clearly defined and unquestioningly practiced, and I wonder how it is that we have moved so far from this. Is this the price of free will? That we should choose a working life so empty, unfulfilling and so hard?

Of course, we have created many different versions of this state of affairs, some people don't work physically hard but exhaust their energies behind a desk. Some are hugely fulfilled but get very little in return. Some earn vast amounts of money but are then completely unfulfilled or even riddled with guilt. The variations are as endless as there are people but how many can truly say they don't work hard and are completely content. Now some might say, there's nothing wrong with hard work and I would agree if it is not damaging to your health then hard work can be very satisfying. Others might say that too much contentment can lead to a loss of drive.

I've heard all these comments before and I believe that most of them derive from the limited constructs that have formed our society today.

What's wrong with coming into life knowing from a very young age exactly what makes your spirit dance with joy, being encouraged and guided in a way that would enable you to make the most of this gift, it being your particular talent, and in return be received with open arms by a supportive community?

I know for most people this would sound simplistic, ridiculous and just a little too saccharine for their taste. This is where I know I've hit the mark, when people feel uncomfortable, when the sarcasm comes out in full flow and the word 'cheesy' starts being bandied around. This is what we do when we take a beautiful idea, crush it and throw it in the bin. We then build yet another big wall between ourselves and the huge empty feeling we have in our heart and try to convince ourselves we're better off without it.

I would like to find ways of choosing better.

* * *

It's time to settle back into my meditation, to prepare myself mentally and energetically. I sense the shadow of the Minotaur creep into view. I don't feel scared or even cautious at this point, I have become used to having it around and have reconciled myself with what I need to do, how to work through and integrate all my demons.

My mind becomes calm and I consider the idea that I believe we all have something to offer this world, like an eight billion-sided crystal. If we were all allowed to shine, the human race would be operating at full potential, each person feeling gratified by the collective enrichment this creates. Although this sounds utopian, I can see no reason why, if we were nurtured this way from birth, we would all want this for ourselves and others, understanding the mutual benefit we would all receive from it.

I believe we are all trying to do our best with what we have on our plate and if you've been served nothing but neglect, judgement and abuse then how would you know how to offer anything else in return?

I sit with this for a while, aware of the many people who are already working hard trying to turn this malpractice around in our society. How can we teach the importance of being kind to ourselves and to each other? When I become frustrated with how slowly this seems to be happening I have to rein myself back in and remember the power of the small combined with the hundredth monkey theory.

And then I remember that we can really only start with ourselves. As I deepen my breathing to engage with this concept I sense the shadow on me darken. 'Good,' I think to myself, 'let's do some work.'

I hear some snuffling about in the darkness and vaguely ignore it. I've nothing to hide. I've written a whole book on my story and being a 'creative', I've more or less covered this. I continue, ignoring the sounds of the shuffling about going on nearby.

'Are you OK over there?" I enquire brightly.

'I'm fine, you just concentrate on yourself,' it throws back at me.

'OK, no problem.' And it is no problem. I was such a lucky child, a free recorder put in my hand at the age of six which I took to immediately. I was told I could learn the clarinet when I reached twelve years of age, but at seven, when my father was told I wasn't too young to learn, he went straight out and bought me an instrument. The uncool clarinet turned into the cool saxophone as a teenager and my desire to impart my knowledge to others meant that I started teaching at fifteen. I seamlessly began work in adulthood as a saxophonist and teacher and inheriting the money for a house without a mortgage at twenty-five put me in the incredibly fortunate position of not having to worry about my low level of income. I was cash poor but property rich, until the age of thirty when I suddenly realised I was doing quite well.

At thirty-two I had my epiphany and although I have

always lived on, what most people would call a low income, I am interested in the fact that it happened in my most abundant phase of life. Although my income had slightly increased, what was more important was that I *felt* abundant for the first time as an adult. It was at that moment that my world just opened up.

I started working with healing, healing myself first and foremost. With the help of some very powerful healers in my life I not only healed my asthma but also a creative block I didn't even know I had. I started writing songs, and I took up the harp to work with sound vibration. Then came the journeys, in the form of talks with my songs and then my book and ... my train of thought comes to halt. At first I'm not sure what it is but then I begin to notice the change in atmosphere. Everything has become very still, no other sound, except the echoes of me rattling on, and the temperature seems to have dropped. The shadow in my presence hasn't changed and yet everything has.

'Hello?' I call. Silence. 'Hello?' I call again. The silence is unnerving and I can't work out if I'm meant to be doing something or to just carry on. I call out one more time but still nothing. I am nervous but I'm caught between my desire to just ignore it and carry on and my need to sort this out. It feels very unpleasant. Normally I would just walk away from this, not wanting to invoke any unnecessary distress or difficulties. Avoidance is usually my chosen path, ratified by some rationale which I tell myself is for the best. But this is just about me, there's no one else to upset or rub up against.

So I get up from the grassy cushion that is my meditation mat for this journey, and brace myself. I only need to take a few steps so that I can see the beast I have been only imagining in my head since I began this journey. Seeing only the shadow and visualising the face to fit the silhouette has been dancing on the edge of my consciousness for a while. It's time to confront it, no more avoidance. What's there to be scared of? With my usual bluster and bravado I turn to see it front on and at that moment a shaft of light reveals its face just long enough for me to see with clarity its distorted form.

I recoil.

I turn away, feeling my breath, like a punch, spring from my belly up into my throat. I'm fighting the tension in my chest and the constriction in my windpipe. My heart is pounding as I try to remember all my breathing exercises and my need to calm my thoughts, but my mind is also trying to grapple with what I have just seen. It was me, for sure, but not how I could ever have imagined, not in my worst nightmare.

'What, who, oh my G-d?' I manage to get the words out but realise my voice is as distorted as the image in my mind I can't seem to shake off.

The Minotaur spoke, its voice as calm as a still lake. 'What's the problem? I thought you said you'd more or less got this covered.'

I slump. Surrendering to it, I regain control of my breath and my mind opens up to a realisation that I had just been bobbing on the surface of my story, like a beautiful white iceberg that glistens in the sun while hiding its dark secrets below.

I need to press rewind and revisit my story but from a place of safety where I can begin to grow accustomed to this new monster in my midst.

＊　　＊　　＊

Where had the schism occurred, between my story and the face I saw, the contortions, the pain, the sorrow? What happens as we go through life?

'What are you talking about?' It takes on the voice of so many people in my life, in all our lives, that laughed at me through the years.

My breath is still tight but my need to face this is driving me. 'I'm talking about what happens to us in childhood.' I'm not looking for pity, I'm just trying to understand the journey.

'You said yourself, you had a great childhood.'

'Yes, and on the face of it, I can't deny that. But that's only in comparison with what we have come to expect.'

'And what is that exactly?'

I note its tone, derision yet again, I've heard it all through my life and from my lips too. Sometimes we can't help ourselves when met with innocence and bright hope.

'We've all been sold the story that life can't fulfil our dreams, that they're impossibilities and it's downhill from almost the moment we've uttered them out loud, as if the very air, the physicality of real life they encounter, crushes their power.'

'But that's the truth.' It closes me down.

'Yes, it's the truth we've chosen to create so we manifest it, we shape the future we expect defined by our expectations, our perceived mindset. It's a collective box we've constructed for ourselves and closed the lid on.'

'You want to break through the boundaries of a collective truth?'

'It's not only me!' my voice has returned to me. 'Just look at a child, up to the age of about six or seven. They are, generally, curious, bouncy and sparkling with potential. I love that energy in kids.'

'Yes, then puberty hits, and it's all over. It's just hormones.'

'I disagree.' I am adamant I am going to remain devil's advocate here (the irony doesn't escape me). 'It's never just hormones, though they play their part of course.' I attempt to get an overarching view. 'I was such a happy child, always giggling, but below the surface there was a complex web of judgmental voices, like a never ceasing undercurrent of commentary.'

'Nothing new there.' It scoffs at me.

'Absolutely no, but my voices weren't damning or belittling me, for being unworthy or just rubbish, like most inner voices, mine were telling me off for being too confident and cocky, for being a show off. I was getting in there, well ahead of everyone else, and policing myself. Oh, I suppose I shouldn't forget that I didn't like my physical looks. That certainly confused things for me. My Jewish nose and black curly hair ensured I always played the wicked witch in school plays. At the time I didn't see it as a racial problem, just an ugly one.'

'And you didn't receive any abuse for being Jewish? It's probing me.

'No, I didn't suffer any antisemitism, so never considered it an issue and never made the cultural connection to why I saw my nose and hair as ugly. Antisemitism was something of the past, something my parents experienced, but not me. I had a different kind of abuse to deal with; my own.'

'For doing what?' It genuinely seems curious.

'I loved talking, telling stories. If I had something to say, I couldn't just say it, I had to paint the whole picture. When I got home from school I couldn't just tell Mum, I then had to tell everything all over when Dad got home. My parents were endlessly patient with me, but my friends got easily bored. So I started telling it quickly before they lost interest and adopted other annoying foibles to manage the uncomfortable situations. But I didn't stop the talking. By the time I was a teenager my self-hate was huge but I didn't, or rather couldn't, switch off my outward energy. I continued telling stories, playing my clarinet, acting and doing well at school, but quietly pulling myself down all the time.

'It's not even as if I was brilliant either, I had internalised Grandma's words ensuring my persona to be that of a B rather than an A student. Over time, as the stories changed, I just became very good at talking myself out of going for anything because I didn't want to look like a show off and by the time I should have been going to university I had replaced this judgemental voice with the voice of my boyfriend and some friends around me so I now believed I wasn't good enough anyway. It was a self-fulfilling prophecy.' I pause for breath.

The complexity I could see in my face, the face of my Minotaur were all the mind contortions of my childhood self trying to navigate the waters of society's expectations. My left brain distorted in size in relation to my right, was vastly out thinking my feeling senses and I was the one who lost out. I was lost, a mind without an inner guidance system, simply following a torch held up by millions before me in a society that had lost its way generations before.

'Phew!' Unfortunately there was no compassion in its voice here, 'Glad you got that off your chest?'

'Well, yes but how do I translate this into a way forward?' I knew it wouldn't respond in a helpful way so I continued before it could offer any more unhelpful, unsympathetic interjections. 'It was Picasso who said, "it took me four years to paint like Raphael, but a lifetime to paint like a child." We need to put the simplicity of life back into our thoughts, both adults and children alike. So we can learn to get out of our own way.'

'That's the truth of it.'

Wow, I thought, it's with me at last.

I couldn't work out if this face I was running away from had looked like this from the start of our journey or had just transformed, creating this grotesque facade, just as I reached this petal. Why do the ones we think are going to be the easy ones always turn out to be the opposite?

It responds to my rhetorical question, 'So where has this left you?' The beast's voice seems a little gentler and if that is just my perception, I decide to go with it anyway. It's easier to proceed that way.

'It left me without a voice.' I stop at the huge realisation of this. Put so simply I am amazed I hadn't seen the clarity of this before, how all roads led here. My asthma was a result of my unspoken grief, but it was multilayered. I was grieving for my mother for feeling unloved, grieving for the loss of my voice. The constrictions I felt in my throat reined in my energy and I found myself standing down. I became a 'backing' vocalist as my voice just had no power. I had a huge dead zone in the middle of my range, around my heart; a fairly unusual place to have one. I stopped taking on any responsibilities in life, feeling I had no authority or anything much of value to offer, which was reflected in what a friend later labelled my 'poverty consciousness'. I only took on supporting roles, always standing behind someone else.

* * *

When I had my awakening and started my healing journey, I gradually began to find my voice as my asthma healed. I found my writing voice, then my speaking voice. The singing voice would be the last to come. We all know that is the most vulnerable.

Only two years after taking up the harp, in 2005, I started singing my songs at the Penny Brohn Cancer Care Centre. There

I met people who were learning to 'live well' with their cancer. It was a profound time of learning for me whilst helping people discover that deep place inside us all where we can heal.

What stood out for me was how many women told me they couldn't sing, or how they had to sing in secret or had been told they weren't allowed to sing as children. These quietly spoken revelations broke my heart. I can only hope that this centre and the small part I played there helped them do the deep healing work they were searching for in their lives.

During my time here, Pat Pilkington, one of the founders of the Cancer Care Centre and wife of the former Reverend Canon of St Stephen's Church, invited me to dinner. She told me how, alongside her husband, they had started doing their healing work in the church decades before, until it grew into a centre in its own right. Pat, now a widow, lived near me when I lived in my village just outside Bristol. I had the honour of getting to know this profound, spiritual teacher and her boundless generosity in the last few years of her life.

Coincidently, at this time I connected with the church. St Stephen's is the parish church for the city of Bristol, first built in 1247 soon after the river was diverted and the city expanded beyond the original city wall. Since it was the first church to be outside the city wall, its patron is Stephen. The New Testament tells the story of Stephen who was the first Christian martyr. He was killed 'outside the city wall' a phrase that became significant and was a pattern to be repeated in other cities.

The first event I attended there was celebrating the installation of a piece of artwork commissioned for the reredos behind the altar. The screen was created on the theme of reconciliation and included an image of Stephen. The church had that ethos at its heart and I felt it profoundly. Naturally I was drawn there, especially to the lunchtime music concerts run by my friend David Mowat.

One time, while playing at one of their many concerts, I was pleased when the current Reverend Canon, Tim Higgins, came to talk to me.

'Tell me about what you do?' he asked. I explained about the work I did with sound healing and out of this conversation came many more. He granted me a good deal of his time over the years, as we would chat over a coffee in the church cafe. I spoke about my new interests in astrology, I Ching and healing and he would translate my ideas and show me how they appeared in his scriptures.

Once he invited me to play the harp for a meditation with the congregation. It felt like the ground was shifting. I was grateful for his open-minded approach with his place in the Church and, in turn, it opened mine. I knew I had to start changing my belief that organised religion was the dogmatic beast in the body of the Minotaur.

When I learned about astrology and chakra energy, I developed the idea that Christianity was limited to the archetype of the evangelist. This is the first stage of the spiritual journey, stepping out of the heart into the throat chakra, speaking its truth. But it had got stuck there. Now I felt as it was embracing the idea of meditation – even if it was only in a few churches – this journey into the third eye showed me how things were changing.

It wasn't long before Pat told me it was her time. After she died, anyone who knew Pat would understand that although her passing was devastating for those she left behind, for her it would be a joyous reunion with her husband, who had died just a few years before.

This was 2013 and I had already moved to Frome but I very much wanted to play at her memorial service which would be held at St Stephen's. Wanting to do my bit to honour the impact she made on my life, I kept in touch with the Penny Brohn Centre about the memorial. However, they told me to contact the church itself. This wasn't always easy as I was aware of Tim Higgins' busy schedule.

With a travelling distance of an hour between Bristol and Frome, my visits to my home city were far less frequent and always tightly packed with work and errands. My visits to the church were few and it could well have been a year since I'd been there. (The last time was when I took Mark for an evening where the Reverend Canon was talking about how he wished to reintroduce a labyrinth, that could be walked as a meditation tool, to the church.)

The next time I was in Bristol, it was a bright summer's day and I had, unusually, some time on my hands. I decided to make my few errands on foot which involved crossing the city centre virtually past the church. It suddenly occurred to me that I could just pop my head around the door without too much of a detour and maybe leave a message. As I walked towards the door I could see Tim sitting in the window of the cafe in a meeting. This meant he was in, but busy. As I got closer I could see that he was talking to my friend David Mowat who coordinates the music amongst other duties at the church. Now there was a chance I could interrupt. As I stepped into the cafe Tim's jaw literally dropped,

'We were just talking about you,' he gasped.

'Oh, how lovely,' I said, 'All good I hope?' We laughed as they went on to explain that they were just discussing Pat's service and how they wanted me to play. As the conversation continued, I was able to share what I'd been up to in the last few months. I explained how I had moved to Frome and then Tim looked at me again.

'So you've just come from Frome today, it's not like you were just passing!'

We all recognised the thought that perhaps Pat had guided us together that day, just to make everything run smoothly.

When the day of the memorial service came I felt very privileged to be a part of it. It was a beautiful event, and I got to know a little more about her work at the cancer centre through the testimonials of the many people who honoured her. Her powerful spiritual teaching helped people who had never considered such concepts, gain an understanding of their illness, in a way that was neither condescending nor off-putting. This new perspective had transformed their lives.

Pat was a huge inspiration. Just to step into her house was like stepping into an energy field of high vibration. I miss her wonderful friendship and how her life, so deeply bound in service, inspired me.

*   *   *

How was I going to bring these inspirational qualities into my life? It was important to remember that humility is probably the most important virtue as I came to understand that service was not about what I considered to be the big things, like my vocational work. Worrying about how good a harpist or healer I could be is the mindset of the ego. A life in service as a human being, is first and foremost about the small things, about bringing Heaven to Earth, and this starts in our heart. If we can learn to be kind and of generous spirit in every aspect of our lives, it doesn't matter what we do or where we do it, if we can bring these qualities into our natural way of being we have discovered our divine purpose.

While I was endeavouring to build this into my daily practice, my new life in Frome was also helping me to dig a little deeper, to discover where to put this energy. I began to see a thread that took me back to the healing group I joined after my awakening.

It was 2001, pre 9/11, and the facilitator convened a meditation on the Middle East, specifically in Israel as the West Bank wall was being built amid growing feelings of concern. The meditation felt very powerful, and I saw an earthquake shudder through the border line. It unnerved me.

That night when I went to sleep, I put up a quiet intention that if there was anything I could do to help I would like to offer my services. I had no idea what that could be or how that could be brought about from my place and capacity in the world, but I believed the universe works in the most amazing and mysterious ways, especially when you don't meddle with the request.

Three years later, I attended a talk in Bristol. It was offered by two men, one Palestinian, one Israeli, they were like father and son. To see two men on opposing sides of a war showing such love and openness, rising above collective anger and fear, was very exciting.

They spoke of how they worked tirelessly in Jerusalem, holding peace gatherings when the violence escalated. They gathered children of all races to show the adults how to be together without violent conflict. They were now taking their work worldwide. *Sulha* means reconciliation, and their optimism and commitment to their Sulha Peace Project was very moving. Their dream of peace was the inspiration behind my song which I have named after and dedicated to their work.

This song found its way into my first album, and I knew it had to have a place in this petal as it holds the energy of service at its heart. If we have no idea what our purpose is or have lost the gift that enabled us to bring it into our life, then I hope you might agree that rediscovering it becomes vital to our happiness and sense of self-worth. Sometimes when we investigate our history we realise we have always been living our purpose, sometimes it is lost deep in our psyche, though there are nearly always clues when you look back through your life. For me it was a slow journey of realisation and healing.

In one way I was lucky, as it felt like I had injected myself with painkillers, and I didn't realise the pain behind the story till after I'd healed it. This is the nature of suppressing pain. When trauma becomes too great, this is what we do. I believed I had a wonderful life, and although I really did, that was the superficial, physical aspect of my life. Deep below the surface was huge ancestral pain that I still hadn't fully uncovered.

Healing this was to be my act of service.

PART 2

Although I had little time and space to breathe, by the autumn of 2014 I sensed I was being guided on a journey that had quite a specific destination, but I just couldn't quite put my finger on it.

I wanted to live a life in service, but the many boulders clogging up my sense of flow meant knowing exactly what to do and how to go about it remained veiled in mystery. I would constantly sway between being absolutely fine with not knowing, to being frustrated for not being able to tune into my internal guidance system. I spent too much energy tugging on the sleeves of others for help, like a child always asking what they should be doing next. And then I'd slip into being in flow with it all again.

Some years back, when I was invited to play my harp in the Peace Dome during the Glastonbury Festival 2010, I received a beautiful guiding hand. I was just starting the *Conversations With God* books and as I sat in the Stone Circle field before the festival began, when everything was still quiet, I began to read. The first thing it told me was that G-d doesn't mind what we do. G-d only cares about *how* we do it. Just as we send our children out to play, we don't mind what games they play, we just want them to learn to do it with kindness. This stayed with me through all my dark moments of indecision and doldrums.

Then, a few years later I attended a workshop with Andrew Harvey, a Sacred Activist. Sitting next to him, in the circle of about thirty, I was transfixed by his passion and energy. He explained an ancient teaching that tells us we each have a divine purpose; one thing that we have come here to do. We may do a hundred things but if none of them are that one thing then it is as if we have done nothing.

This completely threw me. While the ideas from *Conversations With God* gave me solace, these words were like having a rug pulled from under my feet and left me bereft of comfort. I still felt I had no idea what my specific purpose in life was. I was doing too many things to know which I should be concentrating on; which was my one thing.

What saved me was a memory of a workshop I attended on Sabian Symbols at an astrology camp. There are symbols, or revelations, for each degree of the zodiac. I discovered my sun, sitting at eight degrees Pisces, said,

'Summons; A girl blowing a bugle!'

I hear a sound from the shadows but I can't decipher its meaning.

'Did you have something to say?' I am trying not to sound

defensive, though I am still recovering from the memory of the terrible disfigured face I had seen; my face.

'I was just wondering if you were going to elaborate any more on this?' Its tone was almost innocent.

'Yes, it is ambiguous, the insights do generally leave room for interpretation.' I am still trying to relax in its presence.

'And what was yours?'

'Well, I suppose the bugle was my saxophone, but really, I used the saxophone as a surrogate, something to hide behind. Now in the last few years I believe I have found my voice and that this was my purpose. And in turn this has enabled me to help others find theirs.'

'Well, just a little interesting when the last thing you told me was that you felt you had been left with no voice.'

'Yes, but that's the point isn't it?' I am trying not to sound impatient with it. 'The obstacles we create, the pain we suffer, are all because they are specific to us, our special gift that we have lost. Putting our hand in the Minotaur's mouth is worth it because it is the healing we alone need and can do. It's the gold we are seeking.'

I had to rediscover my voice, only because I had lost it in the first place. This was the story that sparked my first book, based on the journey of Paulo Coelho's *The Alchemist* that we have to journey away from home to learn to appreciate and return to what was there all along; the buried pot of treasure.

Now I had found my voice, I had to learn how to use it. A flash reminder of the Minotaur's face entered my mind and I wondered if this deeper reflection on my purpose might make me feel brave enough to take another peek.

* * *

I had, for a while, been engaging with my friend, David, who, as I have mentioned organised the music at St Stephen's Church. He was setting up a course for Sacred Activism. My connections with him were many and always meaningful, beginning in the 80s as musicians, as David is a fine trumpet player. Though our lives took us in different directions, we met again on the streets of Bristol with the 2003 anti-war demonstrations on the City Centre, just a few metres from the church.

As David started working at St Stephen's and brought me in with my harp to the lunchtime concerts, I discovered he was putting on a whole variety of gigs, jams and meetings. This included a political, spiritual, listening group he was designing and leading on behalf of the Reverend Canon. It was called the Reconciliation Laboratory. For me, this couldn't have been more perfect. I tried to keep in touch as much as I could.

We talked quite a lot about what drew us to this church and one time he told me that he had walked to Jerusalem on a personal pilgrimage. This was not long after I had met Johanna van Fessem.

She came into my life on a whirlwind of synchronicity when I was performing my talk *Keys To The Golden City* in the Assembly Rooms on the High Street in Glastonbury, in 2010. When I checked in with the audience that everyone was OK after my somewhat long and technical introduction, a member of the audience piped up and suggested I should write it down. When I said I already had, but that I needed a little help with my book, she told me she might know someone.

I was just sitting down to a cup of tea to catch my breath after the talk, when the woman approached me and asked if I would be happy to meet the editor she was thinking of right now. Within minutes, in walked an elegant Dutch woman.

This is what happens when you connect with the vibration and landscape of Glastonbury and its zodiac energy.

The irony didn't escape me that having put out a call for someone to help me learn to write English, in stepped Johanna for whom English was her second, or even third, language. I hope I didn't reveal my slight embarrassment at this.

Over that first cup of tea together, I showed her a picture I was temporarily using to represent my golden city.

'That's Amritsar!' she exclaimed.

'Well, yes,' I kind of apologised. 'I'm using it generically, as I believe the term "golden city" is just symbolic of our hearts.' I explained that I believed that Jerusalem is the spiritual heart of the world but as we are shifting astrological ages to the golden age of Aquarius, the heart of the world is also shifting. I continued to say that this was all part of my story behind the title of my book *Journey To The Golden City*.

Then she said,

'I walked to Jerusalem on a pilgrimage.'

I looked at her and laughed,

'So you have done this journey!' We knew that we had been brought together for a reason. Her book *Walking Into The Light* tells of her amazing eleven month solo pilgrimage from Holland to Jerusalem. I recommend it to anyone who loves to be inspired by personal endeavours such as this.

The synchronicities did not stop there. When Johanna started to edit my first chapter, my plum tree story, as I had initially called it, she called me almost immediately.

It was inspired by a story of a man who lives in a house in a village in Somerset, with a beautiful plum tree in the garden. Based on *The Alchemist*, one night a man is guided by a dream to walk for three days and nights to receive a sign. As we journey with him, the sign eventually tells the man that there is pot of gold under his beautiful plum tree at home. Of course it takes him the whole story to discover this, just as it took me three days to remember, when I first heard the story, that I too had a plum tree in my beautiful garden in Somerset, helping me to uncover my own Alchemist story.

When Johanna got in touch with me, she explained how she loves to walk and every Equinox, when the sun is moving at its fastest, she packs her bivvy bag and sets off from Glastonbury to walk with the sun for three days and nights. She sleeps out in the open wherever the countryside offers its best shelter. She then told me that on the last Equinox she walked in the Chew Valley, in Somerset and found a stile on the edge of the Mendips where she could sleep.

Well, once again, my heart melted, Johanna had found me before she even knew me. She had camped next to an amazing viewpoint five minutes' walk from my house and my plum tree.

* * *

So now I had two extraordinary people in my life who had taken the idea of a pilgrimage to an extreme in this day and age. As they found peace and reconciliation in their hearts on their journeys to the very heart of the world, their profound experiences of service made me question how else I could play my part. I couldn't walk to Jerusalem but there were alternatives offering the same effect.

Very shortly after I booked onto the Sacred Activism course, David got in touch and told me he would, sadly, not be running it after all. I knew I needed direction, I was never comfortable just floating through life in my watery, Piscean way.

Direction wasn't far away. Within days, my friend Louise mentioned that she was starting an online course of a similar nature, about Sacred Activism and would be happy to meet and discuss certain aspects that she was learning from it. The synchronicity felt amazing as if one was picking up as the other fell away and I accepted Louise's offer. This was a fantastic opportunity to journey with a small group of wonderful people, to pave our path with grit and tears. This felt most timely and deeply sacrosanct.

There were many beautiful offerings. The first was a meditation, using a well-known chant, which invites the sacred creative fire to be wholly met in you. I wouldn't have to wait long for this to come into effect. The second was a meditation connecting to your ancestral line.

When I sat at my altar, a few days after our gathering, I set my intention to be open to whatever wanted to come through me. Almost immediately, I felt a vortex enter my heart. The rush of energy that came from behind was so overwhelming that as it coursed through me, I felt I had to take hold of it, to stop what felt like a gasp of emotion, a huge sob, from my parental line. This did not belong to me but was being passed down to me through my genetic coding. I couldn't ignore it, to turn my back on it would give it power beyond my control.

As I grabbed the blast of energy, metaphorically, in my fist, I heard myself saying,

'That's quite enough for now, I will deal with this later', and I meant it. I'm not sure I was aware of the journey it would take me on. But this was all part of my work in service and I was open and willing.

* * *

That autumn, after the demonstrations opposing the Gaza War, the Frome Friends of Palestine turned its attention to a theatre company from Palestine, the Freedom Theatre, coming to the UK for the first time. They had written a play especially for the tour called *The Siege*. Set in Bethlehem, it is based on the siege of the Church of the Nativity during the Intifada of 2002.

The FFoP immediately jumped into action and offered up Frome as a possible destination for the tour. This was exciting as it was known that they were already looking at Battersea Arts, The Lowry and other prestigious venues. Frome, though small, has two hardworking theatres, both of which are managing to keep their heads above water despite loss of funding following the 2010 elections.

We were amazed and excited that Frome was to be the main host for the area as both Bristol and Bath stepped out of the ring. The FFoP weren't deterred. In the past they had often taken on tasks that look like mountains but always managed to rise to the occasion.

A core group was set up to start fundraising the 5,000 pounds needed to get the theatre company to Frome for one night. The company was only visiting one other town, all the other destinations were cities and we were the only amateur group acting in a three-way collaboration between us, the Merlin Theatre, and the Palestinian theatre company. This was possibly the makings of a disaster, but with so many good intentions I decided it was worth giving it a go and joined the task group.

I instantly had some misgivings. I have absolutely no interest in fundraising and really don't enjoy administration work. But I thought, 'what the hell?' it might be good for me. You never know quite how good it can be, and I was certainly not disappointed.

With all these amazing events going on in my life, as is my

wont, I couldn't resist talking about them to my colleagues at school. I had been working there for many years as a peripatetic music teacher and knew the staff well. After some weeks, Bridget, one of the teachers, decided to speak up. She said,

'I wasn't going to say anything before because I didn't want to worry anyone, but because you've been talking so much about Palestine, I can't keep it to myself any longer.'

It turned out that she was going to be travelling there with her women's football team over the half-term holiday. I was very excited to hear more, while understanding the nervousness her colleagues might have felt for her, and asked if she would come and speak to our group in Frome when she came back.

'This is exactly the kind of event we love to put on, talks about people's personal experiences,' I said. She agreed.

Two weeks later, it's early November and things are as full on as ever for me. Mark's youngest daughter has asked to move in, so I am suddenly dealing with another person in my life with a new role as (self-named) schlep-mum to a beautiful teenage girl and all the chaos that this brings. I also was putting together a new duo with my new found confidence as a jazz singer and saxophonist; another sign that Frome was helping me to find my voice.

The non-judgemental gatherings of a small town jazz scene removed the critical voice that kept telling me I couldn't play jazz. The only way to learn anything is by doing it, if you malign yourself from the outset with judgement, how are you to ever get past first post? This is where I had remained for many years until I arrived in Frome. My Cain had been smothering my Abel for the last thirty years. Here I was being offered some simple, personal conflict resolution.

'So you're now a great jazz musician?' My Minotaur couldn't resist a jab.

'No, of course not, that takes years, but it got rid of many of the obstacles that were preventing me from even stepping on that road.' It was quite a revelation and within a couple of months people in Frome were offering me jazz gigs.

My first was the following weekend and I felt my workload, on top of my already busy life schedule, mounting.

Back in school on my usual Thursday after half term, Bridget is telling me all her wonderful stories and her experiences on her travels to Palestine and I listened with both joy and deep sadness to her tales. When she finished, out of the blue, I said,

'I have been holding on to an image in my mind for the last few weeks,' and I described the image to her. In my mind I saw how Jews and Palestinians, like most warring nations, are just like brothers, one a mirror of the other. My image was of an angry man holding a gun, wanting to eliminate his enemy. He sees two children, in my mind I imagined that one was Israeli and one Palestinian, but both are stripped of their religious garb. How can he tell which is which? Of course, he doesn't want to kill his own by mistake but if they are so similar, why would he want to kill a child that looked so much like one of his own? As I finished describing the scene I flippantly said,

'It could be a play, couldn't it?'

Well, that was it, busy or not, I had set something in motion and it was not waiting for anything or anyone. As I awoke the following morning there were scenes playing through my mind. I had to grab my iPod and speak the flow of words into it before I lost them. Some of the words have been directly transferred into the play from this stream of consciousness that continued to come through me over the next ten days. As I began to write, starting at the beginning and working my linear way through the script, without making any plans or notes, it soon became apparent that a song I had written ten years previously would form the basis for the play.

It was my song, *Sulha*, meaning reconciliation in Hebrew, inspired by the Sulha Project in Israel. It is based on the idea that you have to understand the customs of the people you are dealing with rather than trying to impose your methods on them like the West does.

In the Middle East they work with coffee. You offer a cup of coffee to the table and if it is accepted then you know peace talks can begin. You offer another and then another, the magical number three, and if all three are accepted then you know peace is possible.

Now, a decade later, the realisation that the three cups of coffee would create the structure to enable the process for my Palestinian and Israeli characters to come to their place of realisation and reconcile their conflict, blew me away. The fact that the trilogy kept reoccurring was also something I could no longer ignore, whether it was the Holy Trinity, the three religions at play here or three cups of coffee.

* * *

'It's the sequencing of events thing that gets me every time!' I exclaim.

'But you said you understood the idea of different dimensions?' My Minotaur fires straight back at me.

'Yes, but that doesn't mean I can't continue to be constantly amazed.' I pause for thought. 'I know that in the higher dimensions time simply doesn't work in the same linear way we believe it works here on Earth. But when you receive a little help here and then another piece of treasure there and then it all turns up wrapped up in what seems like a diamond necklace with all the pieces hanging off it like gems, creating one beautiful piece many years later, I still can't help being wowed by it.'

'Well, these are the limitations of a mind driven by the ego.'

'Thanks.' I feel my energy plummet like when you think there's a step but then there isn't.

'We're all human,' it assures me.

'Some of us are only half,' I respond.

It's been a while since I've been caught up in the magic of synchronicity. When you suddenly become aware of the mysteries playing out in your life it can feel like you are being transported into a storyteller's mind. It was a storyteller, brought into the astrology course I attended, and his captivating gifts that brought out the storyteller in me, though it took till I was in my forties.

'But you told me you loved to tell stories as a young girl.'

'I know.' I close my eyes. How did I lose that flame in me? But how wonderful that it was being rekindled once more.

The following Monday, ten days after I had begun writing, 12,000 words later, I placed the final full stop on what I later found out was to be a pretty much complete baby.

'It felt like I had just experienced a beautiful Mozartian-style download of art and guidance all rolled into one.'

'Uh-huh?'

'With all the imperfections of a first time, first draft experience of course.' Even I wasn't that deluded. 'But as I wrote it, it felt like it was writing itself. Each morning I'd wake up with the next instalment playing through my mind. I'd have to reach for my iPod before it disappeared. When I came across a conundrum, a situation that stretched before me without direct input, the answer would come straight into my mind. I described it like making challah.'

I see the shadow of its head tilt in my direction, questioning me.

'It's a plaited loaf, Jewish bread. Breaking bread is a very symbolic part of the Jewish tradition, all traditions, it's even written into the lyrics of the song. *"We'll break bread, not our mothers' hearts"*. I was able to simply tie in all the threads of the storyline as I went. It felt wonderfully easy.'

This is a problem with the conscious mind today, we have lost so much of our ability to simply flow. With each conflict we encounter we invent more and more tricksy ways out, until our minds become like a maze themselves, so many get-out clauses and so much backtracking we have truly lost our way.

'This was just simplicity itself. Effortless and joyful.'

'I am the manifestation,' the beast hangs its head, 'of when you lose the simple way, the uncomplicated mindset. Without this, you are only left with the contortions of the mind, cut off from its source. My body, seemingly, the human beauty and my head, the beast.'

'And there is the paradox. which of you is truly the beauty?' I say. Even with this gruesome image I had in my mind of this beast, my fear was softening once more.

My Minotaur, sensing I was losing my direction, reins me in and asks, 'And the play?'

'Oh, of course, yes I needed someone to read it. I'd never written a play before. I'd studied a few at English A Level, but never the writing aspect.'

'And?'

'Well, this was Frome, I was almost tripping over people. First, I read it to my writer's group I'd joined as I was also trying to publish my book at that time. Then,' I stopped and smiled. 'Well, of course, it just so happened we had some people recently moved into the street. A young couple who were just about to have a baby. He was an actor, just over from living in Hollywood and she was an actor, dancer, singer, hugely influential in her sphere in Canada. As we got to know them, Mark and I did question their choice to come to Frome, but we loved having them as neighbours.

'I met them because a Sicilian restaurant, 200 yards from our houses, had invited us to create an evening of readings, yes, stories, I know, and music. They read excerpts from *The Godfather* to which I played the saxophone and I played harp to an excerpt from Paulo Coelho's *The Alchemist*. And I really had no part in choosing that!' I laugh.

The baby, by this time, was nearly three months old and I was ticking myself off for not having popped in with a present. With the universal wheels whirling as they always do, I stepped onto the street one day and, unusually, bumped into Tamara. We arranged for me to visit.

As we were parting I had a thought.

'Oh,' I said, 'I know you're really busy and everything but would it be too cheeky to ask if you could read my play I've just written? I'd really appreciate some advice on it.'

As soon as I'd said this I tried to retract my words. But she stopped me,

'No. I'd love to read it, what's it about?' When I told her, she reminded me that although her mother was First Nation, her father was Jewish. Not only that, he had worked in a centre for reconciliation in Israel for a year and she had visited him there for a time.

I had to laugh, a laugh full of gratitude and amazement.

As the months flowed on, each person who was willing to read my play or let me read it to them, offered me help and guidance to pull my first draft into shape; some dramatic, some technical, some political. I am grateful to everyone's time and energy, to those that shed tears and those who laughed in all the right places (after a few people had reminded me to introduce the much needed humour). I also have to thank the FFoP and Frome Drama Club for their support and willingness to help me stage it, and the small but wonderfully supportive audience who attended, when the time was right.

The sense of joy, the simple light-hearted feeling of fun alongside the shadows that were lurking behind some of the deep processes I was working through, reassured me that I was working in service, listening to what was being asked and pulling into reality the concept of 'as above, so below'. To be able to pluck the beautiful higher energies and bring them to Earth is something I've wanted to do since I understood it was possible.

Sometimes, I would reach a state of mind when I'd lose my flow, see my journey as completely chaotic and lacking in purpose. Then I would remember these moments of clarity, like fireworks on a misty night, and remind myself that my life has direction.

* * *

I know now that I have to blow my bugle, yet 'showing off' as I saw it then, was something I learned to hate in myself as a child. How would I resolve this apparent contradiction?

Our divine purpose is etched into our knowing, yet no one is taught how to decipher the hieroglyphs these days. It has become such a forgotten art that we have forgotten that we are even meant to discover it. Instead we bully ourselves through our own and each other's lives, playing the game and making sure no one does anything to make us or themselves look silly.

Self-policing is a fabulous chain we all dutifully wear around our necks and heaven forbid anyone should step out of line and remind others of what could be.

The rustling in the background reminds me my Minotaur is never far away, and I acknowledge the fact that I know it's still holding onto the key I need but am too afraid to step up and reclaim. It is mine after all.

'So you know the key is here, why don't you just come and get it?'

With all my heart, I want to blow my bugle, speak my truth, good and loud but there are just so many buts that seem very real and solid to me. Fears, stories and excuses are deeply woven into the fabric of my life. Nothing is as easy as just reaching out and taking it, yet I also know how hard it can be.

'I think I have got myself tangled up with the idea of needing to be a success and worthy of my grandma's inheritance, proving to her that I was right in choosing music, and wanting her to sing our praises.'

'Didn't she?'

'Never to our faces.'

'Some people find that hard.'

I scour my mind for memories of my grandma I can connect to emotionally. My chest tightens and I breathe out. I feel nothing. 'The truth is, that deep down I don't believe I am a success, with or without her approval. That's my beast.'

We all have a story, one we've twisted and changed and built into the walls of our reality. We are all connected, one amorphous beautiful beast, bound up in its profound journey of purpose and healing. And we are all on our way, whether we know it or not, whether you feel you are leading or lagging behind, it is not a competition or a race, we will all finish together and each will find our part to play as the time sees fit.

Although I long for everyone's journey to be filled with joy I know that is not possible or even right, for pain is often the springboard to discovering joy. That is the value of the beast, the beauty that underlies it, and the beast imbedded in what we think is beauty. Nothing is as it seems and that is what makes life so beautifully complex.

Though so many are blind to our divine purpose, it becomes ever more clear that we are all walking our paths the best way we can; a smile in the street, a helping hand, a desire to reach out when the guns are still blazing. It doesn't matter how small the gesture or how great, bringing Heaven to Earth is the way for every person who is breathing on this earth to bring a little more peace into the world.

CHAPTER FOUR

THE FOURTH PETAL: ABUNDANCE

Give us this day our daily bread

Heaven in my Eyes

The caravan is journeying through deserts in my mind,
Sowing seeds along the path.
When it's at its journey's end, I know that I'll find
An oasis in my heart.

One by one, the buds begin to bloom.
Step by step, my heart can beat in tune.

Heaven is in my eyes, now I'm standing before you.
Heaven is in my eyes, I'm finding new ways to adore you,
Reassure you, applaud you.

There are many rooms within the mansion of my mind
Yet I haven't climbed the stair.
When I reach those storeys high I'll throw back the blinds
I know I'll find you waiting for me there.

Step by step, you light up my way.
One by one, you turn my nights to day.

Heaven is in my eyes, now I'm standing before you.
Heaven is in my eyes, I'm finding new ways to adore you,
Reassure you, applaud you.

You are like my golden cup which I can fill with love,
For we are eternally bound.
You are my olive branch and I am your dove.
If you'll be my king I'll be your crown.

Heaven is in my eyes, now I'm standing before you.
Heaven is in my eyes, I'm finding new ways to adore you,
Reassure you, applaud you, adore you.

PART 1

I am aware that I am halfway through my pilgrimage having completed the first three of six petals. In astrology, a midlife crisis is shown when the planet Uranus reaches the halfway point in its journey around the sun. This is called a Uranus Opposition, when you are as far away from your start point and your end point as you can be; the end being the planetary return. As Uranus takes eighty-four years to orbit the sun, this occurs when we reach the age of forty-two, when we are often faced with issues we've so far failed to acknowledge in our lives. It's the time when breakdowns are most likely to occur and many fast cars are purchased.

I have arrived at the fourth petal, the petal of abundance. *Give us this day our daily bread.* I need to tread lightly as I tentatively step through the entrance. This is going to be my most challenging part of the journey. I am, metaphorically, at the furthest point from home, and I need to be gentle with myself and take some time to adjust to my new surroundings.

Before I dive into the meditation, I notice the beautiful flowers that have sprung up in this part of the labyrinth. There are poppies and buttercups and the delicate indigenous bluebells, blending their strong primary colours with the vivid greens. If I drop my eyelids slightly, I feel I am in an Impressionist painting.

I recognise how rare this backdrop is for me; I am usually too caught up in my mind to adorn my house with simple beautiful reminders of Mother Nature and the blessings she constantly bestows on us. Or, worse, I am too worried about needing to spend my money on what I believe to be more important things.

My growing awareness of our disconnection from Mother Earth was revealing to me the void her absence has left in our society and our inability to feel her, and so our, abundance.

* * *

I take a big sigh. Moving to the country had been hugely positive for me; being close to nature in my big garden was healing much of the disconnect, but there was clearly more to be done.

So I decide to start, as I settle back into my process, right at the beginning of my story once more.

Images of lighting candles and the breaking of bread on a Friday night to bring in the Sabbath, with prayers around the family table bring back fond memories. But the feelings of fondness are only in retrospect. At the time, this childhood ritual, didn't resonate with me at all. The prayers, said in a language I didn't really understand (even when the Hebrew words were translated into English), created a distance that I couldn't bridge.

As a I got older, my parents explained that they had brought us up with this tradition so that we could understand our roots and where we had come from. I was always grateful for that and the grounding and stability it brought to my life, but it held no meaning or importance for me. It felt like it was something we were only doing as a duty to those that came before us.

We were perfectly aware that we were living in a fast-moving society where the importance of our ancestral culture was slowly being edged out. But I don't believe we had any inclination of the damage this was leaving in its wake.

I hear sounds in the background, my Minotaur clearly wants to get involved, maybe add some commentary to my rambling thoughts.

I sense a tightness growing across my chest once more and I need to stay calm if I'm going to get to the heart of this one. There are always at least two concurrent voices at any one time, such are the complexities of the ego.

My Minotaur, as if reading my mind, tries to help me out, 'Life is full of contradictions.'

'Yes, and the truth is, I can always see both sides of the story. I know my life is brimming with abundance, I am blessed. And I know that I know it, but then there's always that nagging voice.'

'Saying?'

'You really want to know? The problem is it's so boring, just the usual treadmill stuff. It's the child in me that hasn't grown up and is addicted to things it can't have, things other people have. It's that classic sibling rivalry thing that as we grow up becomes peer rivalry which is much more dangerous as there are no limits then.' I pause to reflect. I think of the material things I choose not buy, mostly for ecological reasons, but then secretly wonder if part of this isn't all wrapped up in my poverty consciousness.

'So what will become of us all?'

'What indeed?'

'You have to remember to be the witness, be patient.' It takes the lead. 'Slow down, all will be well.'

'I love your optimism.' I feel reassured. 'You know, I always thought patience was one of my traits, but I can see myself getting caught up in the frustration. Wanting the answers and having the maturity to understand them only comes with time and a quiet mind; the qualities of becoming an elder. We are currently doing the opposite; determined to stay in the teenage mindset, filling our lives with more distractions and noise.'

'You have stopped listening to your elders, you ignore them and then remove them from society.' It bows its head in contemplation. 'Youth has become king, (like the astrological Leo lion) and instead of shining with an inner sense of self, it has lost its childlike innocence. Sadly the king has become heartless and your culture has become like the self-obsessed teenager. Its physical maturity is in direct conflict with its own lack of emotional maturity having pushed its guidance system for growing up out the door and into the nearest nursing home.'

My energy slumps, we're all just running away from death and getting old.

So when history causes so much trauma that people want to forget what went before and begin to deny their ancestors, what happens then? Because we are not taught to honour our roots and the wisdom that is handed down over the millennia, children start denying their living parents too and all that inheritance becomes lost.

Possibly the saddest repercussions of all this is the stemming of love. I pause with that for a moment, it feels huge. Within seconds my mind moves me on knowing that there is also all the abundance that is no longer carried down through our family line. As we constantly revolt against the generation that came before, thinking we know better, a reckless attribute of the teenage mindset, the links are constantly being cut. Once we have grown up and start to understand the importance of what might have been handed down to us, the sense of loss can be immense, often when it is too late.

I am minded of that wonderfully ironic little quip I heard years ago: 'If only I listened to what my mother told me.'

'Why, what did she say?'

'I don't know, I wasn't listening!'

I had wanted to lighten the dense atmosphere I'd been creating, however unintended, but I wasn't sure if my Minotaur would get the subtleties.

'Are you suggesting I don't get subtlety?'

I stammer a little, 'Well, I'm not sure you'd get humour?'

'I get everything you get and more.' The atmosphere suddenly got heavier, 'Have you forgotten everything?'

I clearly had; and who the teacher is here.

Our tendency is to place ourselves at the pinnacle of our line and believe that everything or everyone that went before is lesser; less intelligent, less cool, less whatever it is we're desperately trying to be.

'No, but.' There are no buts. I give myself an internal rap on the knuckles. Suddenly I am the school child again, feeling small and silenced; by myself of course.

* * *

So what is filling my cup, what have I inherited? I wonder if I should start with my cultural story first?

'Are you listening?' I decide not to beat about the bush anymore and yes, I have a story to tell. I had tried to tell it before but had bottled out. I think I'm ready now?

'I am always listening?' My Minotaur's voice is low but not threatening.

'I know.' I am no longer afraid. 'I want to start at the very beginning but of course, this is just my version. I cannot speak for anyone else.'

'It's important to know the difference between truth and opinion.'

'And all this is about perceived views.' I settle in. 'I am a Jew, but I am English, a woman born in the sixties and it's through this particular window that I view the world.

'I sense that the Jews have always set themselves apart, once they had discovered their own monotheism over the pantheism of the age. They believed that their G-d had chosen them over all other people.'

'Chosen for what?'

'Well, exactly.' I recognise the tangled web I am diving into here. 'This has never sat comfortably with me. I want to be able to say that it is like a mother who favours her children over other people's; that would be a given. But I don't think this is.'

'But the G-d you were searching for was all-encompassing, not just one separate god for each separate race or religion. And not tribal gods trying to claim dominion over all others.'

'Yes.' I collect my thoughts. 'There are many different views but from what I have come to understand, the Jews chose an experience of separation, in a self-determining way, from their G-d and from the rest of the human race.' This took the form of a covenant with G-d.[3]

'I the Lord have called to you in righteousness, and will take hold of your hand and keep you and present you as the people of the covenant, a light unto the nations.' (*Isaiah 42:6*)

When I read the *Gospel of Thomas* it says, in the notes, that the words 'chosen by' G-d could have come out of a translation, from an original meaning of 'separated by' G-d.[4] This intrigued me.

'But you don't know this for sure?' My Minotaur asks.

'No, but once it was planted in my mind, and landed in my belly, a seed had been sown.'

'Can you see what kind of havoc interpretations can create?' Its voice rings like a warning bell. 'Whether it's word of mouth, the media or academia, history books only tell the winner's side of the story.'

'Yes, and Thomas wasn't a winner. His story was buried for 2,000 years. That's why it feels so important that his words have been revealed now and why they feel true to me. Many think his texts were buried like Mary Magdalene's because these two apostles truly understood Christ's teachings.' I feel this energise me.

Many years ago, my brother-in-law introduced me to *The Hermetica: The Lost Wisdom of the Pharaohs*. The book is nearly 2,000 years old, and is based on ancient Egyptian teachings. As I turned each page my heart cried out a joyful 'yes'. There was no hellfire or damnation just insights from an ancient world as I always believed they would have been handed down to us. Wherever this book travelled, society flourished, Jesus was certainly inspired by it. More than ever, we need this book to be rediscovered.

I hear the sounds of a concertina, breathing out its melodies and stories of yearning and joy, pain and pathos. Melodies like yarns, turning the wheel of life, weaving a web of truths and untruths as they are handed down to us. Is it our role to untangle them?

I return to my version of the story of the Garden of Eden, and how it perpetuates through the history of the Jews. A few decades after Christ's crucifixion their temple is demolished and the Jews are forced out of Jerusalem, spending the next years being persecuted and wandering without a homeland.

During this time the Holy Land became a battlefield for the three Abrahamic religions, but there were momentary glimpses of respite in Europe, Spain being the main example, when they all found a way to live in peace.

When Israel was designated a place for the Jews to return to after the horrors of the Second World War, the land was more or less cleared of their Arab cousins, and the Holocaust survivors taken from one perilous situation to another. The simplistic solutions to a complex problem meant that bringing these peoples together, so long divided by conflict, could only be fraught with difficulties.

Amongst the devastation that followed, emerging from the rubble in my mind came a question. Surely, I thought, returning home didn't mean you had to force your brothers and sisters out in the process, the promised land isn't exclusive, in fact I believe the opposite is true. The promised land is where we all find harmony to live together as a family, that's what belonging means. All we have at the moment is more isolation, more walls. Is this being a 'light unto the nations?'

My Minotaur is present, witnessing my words.

'It wasn't till recently, that I heard, that a whole community of American Hassidic Jews believe we are not yet ready for Zionism. They say the scriptures tell us we cannot return to the homeland until we have love in our hearts. When this happens, it will be the second coming.'

Clearly this time hasn't arrived, and too many Jews have returned to the Holy Land before time, with trauma, fear and retribution in their hearts. As the Cold War took hold we find the two opposing super powers using the new Israelis, like pawns, in their war games.

'I do love a happy ending.' I close my eyes.

'Does sarcasm always find its way into your stories?' My Minotaur is calling for a subtle objection.

I nod, yes, objection sustained, a poor slip of my testimonial standards.

'Sadly, I believe sarcasm and sometimes just humour, is often used as a defence-mechanism, when the emotional waters rise. Jews have this down to a fine art. We're all so good at building walls, emotional and physical.' I smile ironically, 'and so that's what the Israelis did. After the Berlin Wall came down it seemed like its ripples were felt all around the world as South Africa and Ireland began working towards change and in Israel there were also some serious attempts at making peace. When they failed, they built a massive concrete wall in the West Bank instead.'

After visiting Israel, I toured around Ireland in the early nineties with a band. I was terrified to experience Checkpoint Charlie on home territory. Seeing young people with huge guns standing on the street reminded me that we were not a nation at peace. Israel was far away but this was on my doorstep. I was that naive. 'But I don't want to bore you with all those stories,' I drop in.

'You think I'm bored of your stories?' It's probing me now.

'Well, it's a thing.'

'I bet it is.' It's really laughing at me now.

My thoughts return to the walls we have built as nations, walls to house out of control bulls, Cold War ideals, religious wars on the home front and now even music festivals. (The Glastonbury Festival 3 metre wall went up the same year the West Bank wall was built).

When I met Jo Berry and her story around the Irish situation, I realised Britain's story, my home just for the past three generations, was also painful and complex.

The more I thought about it the more similarities I could see. When the Celts were pinned to the edges of their homeland, the country was continually invaded from the Romans through to the Normans, and the Britons were no longer the people they once were. Many were scattered far and wide, the Puritans and the Irish to America and the Jews to Eastern Europe and beyond (though they were not just thrown out of Britain).

Those that remained in Britain assimilated and when the country stabilised, having traumatised its indigenous peoples, it started to look outwards and instead of being a nation that was being constantly invaded, it became an invading force itself. It turned its traumas onto the rest of the world. And oh my goodness it was unstoppable.

Two stories, with completely different timelines and geography, but both having similar emotional journeys. What an inheritance I had gained.

*   *   *

My cup of inheritance is rather a turbulent one, so it will be no surprise to you if I say that abundance for me has always been a subject of conflict. I feel both well-off with my house and my comfortable upbringing, whilst at the same time I feel my ancestral shadow is casting a feeling of emptiness over all my wealth.

This also felt true of my British culture as a whole. Despite being an immensely wealthy nation, we are constantly being told we'll never have enough. Our economy has become like the insatiably hungry Minotaur, as we have decreed that it needs to keep growing. We see this mirrored everywhere we look as we keep feeding the machine though it has clearly had enough. Every advertisement pushes this down our throats, instilling a feeling of lack so powerful into our national mindset, that this is what we have created; a debt-based society. Our wealth distribution has grown so out of balance that we are now second only to the US, among major economies, in our income inequality.

This is the paradox in which we live and while I'm beginning to realise that paradoxes are not always a bad thing, I can also see it's something I've juggled with all my life, my charmed existence preventing me from seeing what was lurking in the background of my story.

I was born into a typically middle-class family. I felt I had everything I needed and more, (we don't know what we don't know or what we are missing) and completely understood the meaning of every gift I received. I never intentionally acted ungratefully.

I knew my grandma always hoped my sisters and I would do more with our lives than be artists or musicians. She would often sit each of us down in turn and ask,

'Why do you want to be a musician? Why don't you be a doctor, they're such amazing people'. We had many relations who were doctors, scientists, important inventors and such, but my sisters and I were simply not of a scientific leaning. We were all artistic, and our parents always brought us up with the idea that we should follow our hearts. If we were happy then so were they. That was a very wonderful blessing to have as we went our way in the world but I couldn't help hearing my grandma's words echoing in the back of my mind with every subconscious step I took.

By the age of eighteen, with all these confusing messages going on in my conscious and subconscious mind from my family and society, I rejected further education and ran away from anything that I felt was to do with the status quo. I, basically, winged it through the rest of my life. Looking back, I realised I didn't take on any kind of responsibility or feel any sense of authority in my life, and my income reflected this. With my fully fledged sense of guilt in place – whether it was for eating the forbidden apple or surviving the Holocaust – and feeling that I had enough already, I lived with a permanent sign over my door, telling the angel of money to pass over.

On top of this, my background, whether it was my Jewish ancestry or society's subliminal messages, has taught me judgement. This was something constantly niggling at the back of my mind, pervading my whole approach to life.

When my grandma's money got passed directly down to me I was not only receiving a house but also the chance to live out my dream of being a musician. With the security of a roof over my head I could get by on the small income a musician might expect. Did I think my grandma would be happy with that outcome? The irony was not lost on me and so I decided to live with the idea that in death she would.

However, it took me seventeen years, before I investigated this story properly. I think I was so bound up by its complicated nature I couldn't see beyond my own tightly knotted mind. As my healing journey helped me to let it go, so the story started to unravel. Only then did I begin to associate the onset of my diagnosis of asthma with my inheritance of the house. At first I thought it was just the burden of guilt, of receiving such a huge gift when I know so many have to struggle in life, but I was also aware that this didn't really correlate with the depth of grief that caused asthma.

It was my friend Johanna who, whilst editing my first book in 2010, explained that asthma came about through the relationship with the mother. At first I questioned this as I told her I had a good relationship with mine. Then it hit me that as she did not have a good relationship with her mother and as the inheritance money was passed directly from my grandmother to me, bypassing my mother, so the unexpressed grief was also bypassed. I found this quite astounding and made sense of it by thinking I must have chosen to take on the asthma as part of my healing journey.

Asthma is not a particularly fun thing to have, it is limiting, sometimes painful and sometimes scary. But knowing I have healed it a few times, even though it always returns, I can think of countless far more difficult journeys to choose. Apart from my asthma I am in excellent health and for that I am continually grateful.

As I worked my way through the labyrinth the big melting pot of my inherited emotions was challenging to stir, especially as I only knew my maternal grandmother; my other grandparents all died years before I was born. My mother has little memory of her grandmother, just images of a remote, elderly figure who hardly spoke. The sense of disconnect seems to be a common thread and my asthma was about grieving for this loss.

My maternal line seemed to be all about emotional pain. If I followed this line back, it would take me to the East End of

London and then back to Russia and Eastern Europe. There are no stories handed down about fleeing the Pogroms.

'Would you have wanted to know about all that miserable time?' My Minotaur speaks, it is being gentle but straight with me.

'Never far away are you?' I remarked.

'Not when you're talking about emotions, that's when I am at my strongest, energised by them.'

I knew that. 'In answer to your question, yes I think it would have been good to hear, however distressing. It's the not knowing that lets the imagination create the bigger demons than they often need to be.'

'Yes, and these would have been stories of the survivors.' It dropped this like a lead weight.

Sometimes we are slow to remember these things. It would be another few years before I would look at the many great uncles and aunts, on my father's side, who didn't leave Europe to meet their probable demise in the Holocaust.

I pick myself up. 'Shielding us from pain is what has created the troubled mental state of our country today. We must learn to speak of the pain. All we do is suppress it and then there you are, bigger and uglier than ever.'

'I beg your pardon.' It is clearly put out.

'You know what I mean, it gives you power, you just told me so.' The silence confirms I have spoken its truth.

'But your family did well, your grandma should have been very proud of herself.'

'Yes, she did well,' I sit with this for a moment. 'She was self-educated, extremely well-travelled and very interesting to talk to. She was a successful businesswoman and loved by many. But, it was not without its price.'

'But?' My Minotaur knew that wasn't everything.

'But ...' What was it? 'To me, as a direct descendant, I felt no warmth. She was so critical, there was never any praise (except to others, ironically). If you were foolish enough to ask for her opinion about something you had done or wanted to do, the long silence that followed while she wrestled with her thoughts, said it all. Yet she would have been devastated if she felt she had offended. I knew that silence, it was in my inheritance package. She couldn't wrap you up in hugs, verbal or physical.' As my only grandparent it took decades for me to fully understand what I had missed.

To break the cycle I knew I had to start putting certain changes in place. I had to trust that my grandmother had released all her limiting emotions in death. For me, they were still hard-wired into my genes.

I wondered where all this left me. I had built up a huge store of creative gifts that I wanted to offer the world; my music, talks, books and plays, all bound up by some kind of restricting forcefield, holding me and them back. I felt like a fortress full of treasure struggling to let the drawbridge down. Thankfully, the breathing mechanism that was causing my asthma was helping me build the image and the resolutions I was searching for.

*   *   *

I was so caught up in the unravelling of this story, I realised I was completely ignoring my father's lineage. Much of this was to do with being told that asthma comes from the mother, however, I was missing a vast part of my history. Maybe this was why I could heal the asthma but then it would return.

My father's family were West Country Jews, coming in from Romania and Russia, around the turn of the century, in a roundabout way to Wales and then Bristol. Unlike my mother's side that arrived in the Capital and found wealth with hard work, my father's parents did well, but were certainly not wealthy. This wasn't helped by the fact that my grandfather had a hole in the heart and died when my father was fourteen, two years before the Second World War began.

My father never spoke about it as a big thing in his life, he just told me how he still talked to him on a daily basis. His life was a constant honouring of the musical and artistic talents he, and we, had gained from his father. Whereas my mother seemed to spend her energy trying to shake off the negativity bestowed upon her by her mother, my father only spoke positively about his. That was his view on life, and he imparted it wherever he went, helping my mum shake off her lack of belief in herself and develop her talents as a writer amongst other things.

Interestingly, Dad was told all his life that he was a healer. This terrified him and he spent his life running away from this truth. What he couldn't run away from was his in built ability to heal in every moment so that he lived ninety-three years in full health till his last day. When I finally 'got it' and stopped hassling him to look into these skills, I felt deeply humbled. It is the highest form of service, I believe, to heal yourself in a way that naturally helps all those around you to heal. This is like the Hawaiian Ho'oponopono healing method.[5]

Although he did pass his healing abilities onto me, I also believe we all have them if we wish to open that door. Sadly, though, I continually block it, like I block so many of the gifts I am offered in life. I am having to learn to receive the hard way.

So for many years, I felt in a state of balance, thinking I had my positive aspects from my father's side and the negative from my mother's.

'And what happened?'

The words startle me though I certainly should be used to my Minotaur turning up by now. 'What happened? I'm not sure. I think it just slowly crept into my consciousness as I travelled on my healing journey. Then, one day, I made another of my classic mistakes.'

'What do you mean classic?' It asks.

'With my dad, it's always about money. My father always carried a sense of contentedness and that was inherent in his life. He always lived well. He was immensely generous to us, but he simply never had a good relationship with money outside his family. Ironically that never bothered him, I somehow took it on myself. I always had a completely naive take on money, still do. If you have nothing to hide why shouldn't you talk about it?'

'What did you say?' Its voice has deepened an octave like it's trying to calm the oncoming storm.

'Well, first you need to know the background. It started when I told my friend how much the boat my dad had recently bought cost. I must have been about twelve.' I still have an underlying innocent feeling about this, like 'what did I do wrong?'

'And what had you done wrong?'

'You know, you don't talk about money with other people.' I stop. 'There it was again that tightening in my chest. To be told off by my father, even though he literally just pulled me aside and told me quietly and gently, mortified me. I had let him down. That feeling never left me and that fear of talking out of line always silences me. Unless, if I'm feeling confident, then I'm off, speaking twenty to the dozen.' I laugh. 'You see what I'm up against in myself.'

'The paradoxes abound.'

We are almost laughing together now, but then I bring myself to a halt. 'But you see, there's so much complexity tied

150

up with Jews and money.' I try and imagine what it would have been like living as second class citizens for centuries, not being allowed to do any jobs except the ones that no one else wanted; the tax collection, for instance. The Jews were hated for it, well who wouldn't be and when that's all you can do, you're going to get pretty good at it. And then you became wealthy by it and so were hated even more. It's so ironic when I think of all the poor Jews living like peasants in the Shtetls in Russia, selling their wedding rings for loaves of bread in the war ghettoes, and fighting for workers' rights with the unions when they arrived in America.

The concertina effect squeezing the very breath out of our lives historically still fascinates me. I contemplate the beautiful harmony that existed between the three religions in mediaeval Spain that then created a huge backlash with the Spanish Inquisition. Then later, the assimilation of the Jews in Germany and their contribution in the First World War culminating in the restrictions on where they could work being finally lifted. We all know about the backlash that occurred after that.

But I know that people only see what they want to see. There are rich and poor Jews just as there are rich and poor Christians and Arabs. We are all anything and everything but if you have a bug to bear you can find whatever you're looking for in every type of person or race.

'Seek and you shall find.' This falls like a teardrop on my words.

This money issue was bigger than anything I had examined before. And because of its size, I couldn't see for looking. Once I had recognised the enormity of the shadow bearing over my father's line, suddenly I could see the light shining from my mother's. For the first time I really felt the positivity and the ease in which money flowed through this side of my family, allowing me to fully receive my house as an inheritance free of guilt.

The last time I had to deal with my father's uptightness when talking about money, in adulthood, I decided to try humour. I was in my forties. Dad started to chastise me for talking too openly about money once more, so I decided to burst the tension with, 'but just maybe you should stop being so anal about all this!'

I'm not sure my father laughed but my mother and sister, who were also present, certainly did. Looking back I'm not sure I gave him the chance to respond, but it certainly helped me.

Humour was always the best way for me to break through resistance, it worked every time. The root chakra reference would also become a bit of a theme.

PART 2

As 2014 came to a close, the next year started with much to do and busyness at the top of my agenda. I was still travelling to Bristol regularly for lessons and gigs and visits to family and friends. Now I was building up a similar life in Frome but with this extra job of being part of the team that was bringing the Palestinian Theatre Company to my new home town.

What I hadn't considered was how I would discuss this with my parents. Since I had joined the Frome Friends of Palestine a year ago I knew just mentioning the name of the group would cause tension. But I was talking about it so much generally, it was hard not to bring the subject up. However, I had been here before with my whole spiritual journey and had learned to button my lip and only mention it when the time was right.

One gift that came along to break the uncomfortable nonconfrontation was the fact that my parents were trying to sell their building. They had spent the last thirty years in a fantastic penthouse on the top of their five-story warehouse, complete with tenants, in the heart of the Bristol inner city area of St Paul's. It was Dad's mission to relocate to somewhere smaller. Now in his nineties, he had wanted this sorted for many years, so he wouldn't leave mum with the burden of maintaining the warehouse. However, the economic climate hadn't allowed it to happen till now and at last there was light at the end of the tunnel.

With this in mind Mum was starting to clear things out and Dad was doing his usual offering of stuff he'd had hoarded away for years. Although he knew we never would want any of these things he still kept offering and we kept saying no. It was like a little ritual went through. One day when we were enacting these roles once again, I remembered that the FFoP were hosting one of their famous biannual jumble sales. This one was to raise money for the theatre company.

'You could always donate this stuff to the Palestinian jumble sale,' I said knowing I was poking a hornet's nest.

'Julius,' my mother called out, 'do you want to give this to the Palestinians?' I can't remember what my father said in reply, but I remember holding up my hands in defence and telling them they absolutely didn't have to if they didn't want to.

It wasn't long before my parents agreed to give their cast-offs to the jumble sale along with their assurance that I hadn't pressurised them into it. When I arrived with the goods at the church hall, I made it known that they had come from my parents and the gesture was respectfully honoured.

Another tricky subject to broach was my play, a new venture for me. My sisters and I had always followed in my father's footsteps. I remembered a wonderful moment about ten years before when my father mused one day how delighted he was that his three loves, his art, sculpture and music had been taken up by each of his daughters, in that order. I was amazed, I'd never thought about it in such a simple, but obvious way. It was beautiful and I really felt his joy in that.

For my mum things never seemed that simple. After having three children she was aware of a lack of continuity in her education having been evacuated during the war. As an adult she decided she would like to do some more studying. With Dad's usual laid back positivity he responded to her 'do you think I could do an A level?' with just, 'anyone can do A levels.' What was great about Dad was that he didn't feed your ego, he just laid the carpet out for you, giving you no choice but to feel positive about yourself. This came naturally to him because he was just conveying what he felt was a simple truth.

My mum was the academic, fascinated by philosophy, politics and sociology and so off she went. Three A levels and a degree later, mum went on to write a non-fiction book about the history of the square in which they lived. Then she wrote a play. This was based on the real-life characters she uncovered in her research for the book. Both were incredibly well received. How could I not talk about mine? I always told my parents everything.

'How could you not?' I sense I am being gently teased. My Minotaur is never far away.

'So, when my mum said she wanted to come and see it, of course, I was slightly apprehensive. It pulls no punches.'

'So, what did you say?'

'Well, it was a process. First, I said they must read it. It is pretty contentious. But then I knew we would have to have a few conversations about it before that.'

'And what did they say?'

'They said they'd be happy to read it whenever I wanted to send it.'

I needed a strategy, to arrive at a place where we would all feel comfortable addressing this uncomfortable subject.

I realised that this wasn't completely uncharted territory for me. I had already covered some difficult ground with my parents a few years before. This took me back to 2010 after I had discovered what I believed to be the cause of my asthma.

One weekend, at a camping party, a few of us were doing some yoga stretches when a child I had only just met the day before looked me straight in the eye and said,

'You look like a witch.'

In the first instance all my memories of hating my looks as I was always cast as a witch in school plays came flooding back, but then, just as quickly, I replaced them with my belief that I am a healer which is, I feel, synonymous with being a witch. Something I feel proud of.

So I replied with, 'thank you, I *am* a witch.'

'I love you, Vicki.' Came the reply. I was stunned. I don't think I had heard those words before so simply stated. A response was required. I braced myself and said 'I love you, too.' Another first for me.

On the way home I had to call in to my parents and as I left I felt I had forgotten something; I had.

A few days later, I found a reason to go back and armed with this sweet story of this four-year-old child declaring his love for me on the most innocent of levels, I was able to bring up this, until now, unspoken issue. I told them how a few of my friends were losing their parents and I how I wanted to tell my parents how much I loved them before it was too late. It was a huge moment for me, speaking this universal, but silent truth.

I had spoken about this with another friend and about how there is a gap, a space between us when we kiss our parents, like the void is too big, too unfathomable to enter. I was amazed at how it only took a deep breath and a conversation and what occurred after that was a slow relaxing of the learned behaviour of the past. Soon we were hugging properly.

'Why had that been so long in coming?' My Minotaur interjected.

I asked myself this many times, but I know we can only be ready when we are ready, when a light is shone on the issue and we have the eyes to see it and the ears to hear. We don't know what we don't know and if something is always done a certain way then that's how it continues till someone decides to break the chain.

Armed with this success story I believed that I could discuss my play with my parents with a positive outcome, but I knew it would have to come in its own time.

*   *   *

Conflict is something I have worked hard to avoid. Over the years I have honed this down to a fine art, so opening this subject with my parents was huge. Of course I still had a long way to go, but at least now I was beginning to notice how often I step away from engaging in challenging discussions. But awareness is the first step towards change.

Soon, I found myself having many conversations discussing the dependable and stable nature of older people as opposed to 'the children of today.' Each time, I smiled and nodded in agreement, until one time I felt the need to pull myself up and I started gently disagreeing with people. I began saying that although this is exactly how it looks, there was something far deeper going on that we as a society are missing.

I began reviewing the lives of the past few generations, the stiff upper lip that the British held so dear to their hearts was just another way of ignoring the deep psychological pain we were carrying as a nation and a culture following two horrific world wars. No one had any idea how to deal with, or speak about, the traumas endured. So many families lived with the heavy, festering silence that remained. Emotions were kept hidden in closets like dark secrets or brushed dispassionately under the carpet.

This is a huge burden the older generations have been handing down to their children. The love that we crave from our grandparents and those before them has been crushed and replaced by a bitterness; emotions that had become hugely distorted.

This is absolutely not about blame, but an attempt to unravel the story so we can heal the deep injuries that we all carry. Our inability, as a culture, to understand what is truly at stake when we fail to help people deal with psychological damage, has created a legacy of impoverishment. The emotional void that this leaves exactly represents how the Minotaur works and keeps growing.

With each shadow that is cast over our society, each new generation, screaming to release the suffocating emotions that their parents cling to, has its own revolution. But revolutions never change anything unless the healing has been deeply processed, otherwise you just replace one reaction with another.

Now, instead of helping teenagers to grow up and out of their mindset; one of extremes, angst, and a lack of any sense of humour, I feel we have, as a culture, simply joined them and become teenagers ourselves.

The younger generation, I believe, are now finally processing all the pain that their forefathers have battled with but lost. As we are now preparing for this great shift for all humanity, I was told from the beginning, that the children would lead the way. The only way to step through into a new awakened sense of self is with your heart wide open.

This is a truly immense task. To open your heart, you have to feel everything. Our society functions with its heart held tightly shut. So the young are literally feeling all our pain for us. No wonder they are struggling. I find the exponential increase in intolerances to food and life in general deeply distressing. The emotional pain young people carry has led to more self-abuse, cutting, suicide and eating disorders than ever before.

Of course this isn't out of the blue, it's just been building gradually over the decades, and as I gradually gained my own sense of this, I soon found others who understood it more fully, calling it Collective Trauma.

What I find extraordinary is how easily we forget that the walls we put up to protect ourselves from feeling pain, also stop us from feeling any of the good things. We end up feeling, what's the song? *Comfortably Numb.* And for many people, their preferred state is an existence much like the feeling of dehydration; the longer the walls remain standing the more our body forgets there is anything behind them. Although the walls were built out of an intelligent response to trauma, it keeps us separated from our knowing, our inner wisdom.

It is time to bring the walls down, but not with anger or revolutionary force. Something evolutionary; something more gentle. Maybe like Joshua's trumpets at Jericho?

'And how are you going to do that?' It has emerged again from the depths of the inner sanctum of the labyrinth. 'Is this you, blowing your bugle?'

'You may well laugh ...' I trail off. Somewhere inside me I

knew I could find the answers I was looking for. Tapping into and reclaiming this lost wisdom would help me regain my sense of self, my authority and sovereignty.

'The thing is,' I persist, 'that all the signs point me there. Even down to the idea that we have forgotten the power of sound. We know that choirs have been springing up everywhere, gently and joyously bringing down barriers between people. We are learning that it breaks down tumours, opens our hearts and is even thought to have built temples in ancient times. It's so powerful and it's free. Sadly as with all these radical ideas, it's become a political thing.'

I have always been politically minded, but the politics in my head and the politics in the real world always seemed light years apart. Now, in Frome, I found a new political landscape, people and movements that I could relate to, shaking the foundations of the walls I had put around myself. Maybe I no longer had to protect my utopian, so called 'unrealistic views', from the cruel, outside world.

Only months after moving to this independently minded town, with its new independent town council, there was an interesting television interview with Russell Brand by Jeremy Paxman. This was like a light bulb moment for me and showed me that what was going on in my head was now also happening in the outside world. He was talking about grassroots politics, the growth of people power but wouldn't rise to Paxman's constant insistence to know what this would look like. Brand responded with the significant words 'I don't know,' and went on to explain that it would emerge in its own unique way and was too big to limit with his personal ideas at this early stage. It felt like a new beginning, something that I could at last connect with, something that was growing all around me.

* * *

I was becoming politicised and an activist, but all this takes time and energy and the combination of all this meant that I started developing back problems. The first time, I pulled a muscle after sneezing too hard.

I hear my Minotaur in the background, 'Don't laugh,' I call out. I managed to get it sorted with a few massages. But the second time it got so bad that when I played my saxophone the pain turned into nausea. I finally dug out a back therapist.

The therapist, Peter Scruby, who is more like a magician, and conveniently had a clinic in the next street, told me I had an inch and a half pelvic twist. Now I am no expert but that sounds like quite a lot to me. He soon put me to rights and then asked if there was anything else I would like to investigate and here I was, full circle back to my asthma.

I must have tried most alternative medicines over the years, as they have come into my awareness, so I thought another angle couldn't hurt. As he began to work on my lungs and back I became aware of the huge resistance I was holding onto in the muscles either side of my spine in the small of my back. I am of a small build and I have always carried heavy musical equipment and never had back problems till now.

I realised there were two stories going on. Frome and all its enticing 'to do' list was certainly the reason, pulling my work/play balance out of alignment. But, having ignored the signs the first time, I was now being offered the lesson again, and the reoccurring back problem was highlighting a deeper issue that was, until now, hidden from me.

The resistance I was holding in my back, felt very tender and deep rooted, asking to be examined. When I was told that the two sets of muscles in the small of the back control our breathing, it wasn't difficult to see how this was deeply connected to my emotional story.

Because we, as a secular society, no longer view ourselves as multidimensional beings and only recognise the flesh and blood, we have created a feeling of loss in the very core of our being. This lies at the heart of our personal wisdom, our power and well-being; a true lack of abundance.

Around this time, someone told me about a connection between our hips and our jaw. This began a series of memory lightbulbs in my mind as through my life I have developed problems in both areas.

It began, after my asthma diagnosis, with my jaw. The first time I was, fortunately, at my parents. I yawned and my jaw locked open. They rushed me to hospital. My mum sat with me as there was a bit of a wait and my jaw become very tense and painful, with a good deal of dribbling.

We were trying to keep it light, but my mum's anxiety got the better of her and twice had to be asked to sit down and be patient.

The white walls of the old hospital felt cold and unkind. Eventually, the doctor arrived and released my jaw, explaining that there had been two near deaths which was the reason for the delay. Deep breath, Mum and I suddenly felt hugely grateful. Just before the doctor ran away, I asked what I should do to prevent it happening again, the doctor replied facetiously,

'Don't yawn.'

We thanked him for nothing and left.

A year or so later I was in the middle of France with Andy, visiting my old school friend, Jane. One day we went to visit some of her friends, at a house deep in the French countryside.

I yawned without thinking and for no apparent reason my jaw stuck again. I ducked into a corner, covering my wide open mouth with my hands, not knowing what to do. Everyone stopped and I pointed to my jaw and made some incomprehensible sounds. Andy, having heard the original story, explained what was going on and immediately our hosts, who just happened to be from Bristol, started giving me instructions.

Amazingly, they not only knew exactly what was happening to me, but also how to solve it.

'Down and round,' they kept insisting. Somehow I managed to grab hold of my bottom jaw and follow their instructions. It worked.

Feeling extremely relieved, I couldn't help thinking that once again I was being looked after as I was with my first experience of asthma. I was nowhere near a hospital and had no idea what to do. Here were two angels guiding me through.

I was also becoming aware that I could no longer read on a beach lying on my front. My back wouldn't bend comfortably any more. At the time I thought little of it but twenty years later I was rightly questioning why I should suddenly lose my flexibility whilst still in my twenties.

Twenty years later, in 2011, 1 had a deep tissue massage. When the therapist got to work, she revealed huge boulders of agony lurking in the bedrock of my arse. (Apologies, but I haven't yet found a better word.) The massage was something I entered into willingly, a fitting gift in return for digging out a compost loo.

These new pieces of wisdom all pointed to one story. I had been holding onto the fear and pain of detachment at such a deep level, I was unaware of it. I had only been looking at the symptoms and trying to prevent them and certainly wasn't putting the pieces of the jigsaw together or digging deeper to find the causes. The asthma became the focus of my need to heal but actually all these physical issues needed addressing if I was going to get to the heart of it.

I began to see my life, like the story of humanity, as a series of opportunities to wake up, to choose the shadow or the light, fear or love. Sadly, with no guidance or real understanding of what was going on, I always chose the former, without realising what was happening. It was time to put my hand into the shit to sift out the treasure.

By 2015 I realised I hadn't seen or even heard from my friend in France for a good few years. Despite the distance in miles our friendship has always remained close. After a bit of insistence I finally managed to get a response from Jane and a date to meet, when she was next in England. We had an hour to catch up, as her time is always understandably stretched between the four generations of her family. I also needed to make sure I hadn't done anything to upset her, as I had grown a little paranoid as the years of silence passed.

Over the buzz of a noisy cafe, I listened while my friend explained how she had been struggling with some difficult events in her life. It dawned on me that I had been blaming myself for her lack of communication. As it is often the way, it was nothing to do with me.

I told her all about my new life in Frome; the stressful and the wonderful. I spoke about my physical problems, and how I had only just become aware of the huge tension in my arse I had been carrying all these years.

Anyone who knows me, will hopefully think of me as someone who remains calm in a crisis, very forgiving and generally easy-going. However, those that know me well will have experienced my uptightness over the silly little things, the slight OCD (Obsessive-Compulsive Disorder) and an ability to be unmoving when I feel I need to be. I try not to let myself be irritated by the fact that this can all be found in my astrology chart, as is my need to connect to my physical body, working in service for the good of all.

So, as I explained my revelations to Jane, she just laughed and, echoing my jibe at my father, said, 'You, anally retentive?'

I must have looked at her in horror, as if to say, how dare you reveal my truth like that. Jane laughed again with that infectious giggle I know so well and warmly replied, 'Don't worry, Vicki, I'm full of shit!'

My face relaxed and my fear of being unfairly judged melted away. I always relish in the knowledge that sometimes there are people you simple can't hide from. I have known Jane for forty years and I value feeling safe enough with someone to be fully vulnerable, to acknowledge your flaws and be able to laugh about them.

*   *   *

My river of abundance still seemed silted up, but at least I felt that I had got my feet dirty trudging through its muddiness. Maybe I could take some core samples?

I remembered an amazing dream, one of many, I had earlier this century. It began with myself as a teacher in an empty classroom and another teacher running in and saying, 'The whole of the Southern hemisphere is marching on the Northern hemisphere. Quick, we have to get out!' I replied, 'If everyone's coming north then we'd better go south.' In my mind I knew we instantly had to get out of the pandemonium that was about to explode onto our world and in that same instant we were immediately transported to the deserted plains of South America.

As the refugee crisis in the summer of 2015 took hold, ten years later, our industrialised nations were being confronted with desperate people who were landing on our shores and I recognised the prophetic nature of my dream. As the majority of us witnessed this on our screens, people's hearts were either being ripped open or encased even further in steel.

I looked at the rich in our society and saw how ridiculous the divide had been allowed to grow. I would see myself as not so well-off, as my income, limited by my mindset, was so small. Yet, I knew I had more than enough to live a contented life especially when I compared my life to those who were living in poverty here in England.

As we began to see refugees arriving with what seemed like nothing, some arriving with less having lost loved ones during their traumatic journeys, I knew I was as rich to these refugees as the super rich in our Western world seemed to me. I was also acutely aware that this was the story of my forefathers arriving here over a century ago.

I sensed a need to relate our own feelings of wealth to how benevolent we feel towards others in our community as being crucial when it comes to the movement of money in our society.

If you see money as simply an invention, a trading tool, it becomes just an energy that flows in and out of our lives. When we feel our lives are empty, then financial wealth will never fill the emotional pot even if we have billions in our bank accounts. For many, facing the Minotaur with our emotional fears seems more terrifying than coming to the realisation that money really isn't the answer. So we continue to be driven by financial endeavours, keep pushing that boulder up the hill, even though when we reach the top, we know there will be another hill waiting for us. Until we are willing to simply leave the boulder where it is and find another act of service that will fill the emptiness, we continue to fuel the huge corporate engines of Capitalism, while we keep blaming them for our unhappiness and they continue to make sure we never feel we have enough; a perfect storm.

The reality is there is no 'they'; it is all 'us'.

As long as we choose to remain distracted and disconnected from Mother Nature, the monetary regime we cling to will keep us in its grip. We, in turn, will continue to hold ourselves to ransom, giving away all our power. Our emotional intelligence will remain a distant realm along with all the spiritual guidance that is held within these vibrational forces. This is our true cultural and ancestral wealth, our feminine wisdom, something we have turned our back on for centuries.

'So here I am, face me.' Its voice is loud and clear, inviting me to find my courage again.

'I know, I know. But I am worried that you might turn into the three-headed monster, one for each of the petals I'm really having trouble dealing with.'

'Only three?'

'Thanks!' I feel rebuked again.

'But I, the monster, am here for your own protection, safeguarding you from wisdom you are not ready to engage with. This was the serpent in the Garden of Eden. Even though it had your best interests at heart, you have given it a bad reputation ever since, blaming it for where you are today.'

'But that's what we are taught as a society.' I am getting defensive.

'And then you consciously choose to discard these stories,

forgetting that without the proper investigation, they are still in your subconscious, subliminally feeding your conscious mind. That's dangerous stuff.'

'Don't I know it and what's more I, personally, pick and choose which stories are going to need full investigation, and which I think I've sorted.' I laugh, (at myself of course). 'I thought it would be easy with Service and I was very wrong. Now I'm terrified to attempt to see my "Abundance" face.'

'So why are you here, then?' It throws down the gauntlet.

I sigh, but it is a resigned release of energy knowing that I have given myself no choice. It too knows my answer and steps forward so I only have to look up. Surely I've done enough preparation?

As I raise my eyes and behold what stands before me, I feel my eyes well up with tears. The face is emaciated and void of emotion, hopeless. It doesn't terrify me like the last encounter but I am left feeling bereft. I sit and sob for a while.

*　　*　　*

I saw a river cut off from its source, a baby separated from its mother at birth, a flower plucked from the soil. I know this source, this infinite realm of love. I have been lucky enough to have experienced a little taste of its magnificence at significant, but fleeting, moments in my life. As it quickly passes, learning to live without it is something I've had to deal with. However, I am very aware that it is a completely different feeling of lack from never having experienced it at all; these two states of being are incomparable. For me, just knowing that this perfect state of pure love is there, even if I can't hold on to it, keeps my heart and mind in a constant state of optimism and joy.

What upsets me is that I still feel I am living in a state of lack because my ancestral coding, that sits firm in my subconscious, keeps telling me that this is how it is. Labelling my 'poverty consciousness' enabled me to pin it down so I could begin the process of shifting it in my body; recognising as it manifested into the physical stresses I still carry in my back.

I let my mind rest on the image of my dispirited inner beast. I hadn't until this moment contemplated its horns, which were very present. It pains me still that this outdated prevarication about Jews having horns still holds true for some people. This came about from the split between Judaism and Christianity. It was believed that if you didn't accept the new word of G-d then you were with Satan. This fills me with grief. A whole new branch of our cultural family was cutting itself off from its ancestral roots and turning the knife in the wound. Our inheritance remains unresolved today.

My Minotaur's beleaguered face distressed me. How could I begin to heal this suffering? After millennia of pain and loss, we have become mere shadows of our ancestor's glory and yet I am greatly aware that it still shines deep within us all.

There was still so much work to do, in fact the further I travelled on this journey the further I felt from home. Still holding on to my two parallel stories, not only did I have my personal and Jewish story to heal, I also needed to reconcile the differences I saw in our Western culture. How can we begin to breathe life into the hearts of those who believe there will never be enough, those that have an addiction to stockpiling money they can never spend in many lifetimes, and those who are stuck in extreme poverty?

I watch those who have lost all respect for their elders and recognise how this is tied up with our impoverished mindset.

I have never understood the idea of having a prejudice against, and a desire to discard, the very people in our society that we are going to become. The ironies are too huge to ignore, and I feel there is great treasure here if we should choose to heal this generational rift in our culture.

These rivers of abundance have been silted up for too long. The movement of money in our society is like a pyramid, where money flows up and stays stuck at the top. If we chose to change all this, it could flow like a torus, like a tree or a ring doughnut, a universal model that is in constant motion.

Abundance is literally there for everyone as we are all blessed with the same life force. Tony Benn said, 'If we can find the money to kill people, we can find the money to help people.' We just need to believe this and learn to breathe again in a way that will bring life into this idea.

Breath is the gift of life. Like a never-ending love affair, when we breathe in we receive the love Mother Nature bestows upon us and we return the gift in gratitude when we breathe out; it is the Holy Spirit.

I do believe the whole universe is patiently waiting for us to open our awareness to this and plug in. There is enough for all. As I sit and meditate on this beautiful truth, the gratitude that pours from my heart and informs my brain slowly starts to rejuvenate the image of my Minotaur. A glimmer of colour seeps into its emaciated cheeks and its eyes flash a little colour back at me.

CHAPTER FIVE

THE FIFTH PETAL: FORGIVENESS

And forgive us our trespasses as we forgive those
who trespass against us.

Forgiving

'I forgive you' she said, for they know not what they've done.
'I forgive you'. Thought they hold the smoking gun.
She looked up and smiled though she was grieving for her child
I forgive you.

Who's the winner, when they cry out for their blood?
Who's the winner, when the stream becomes the flood?
Those that have no claim cry for justice, in whose name?
There are no winners.

There are those who find deep within their hearts
A wholeness which we're all apart.
We're brothers and sisters that we can embrace.
Would you cut off your nose to spite your face
Hold your hands up for peace.
It's a human race.

I forgive you. It's not an easy thing to say.
If you forgive me then we both can find our way.
It's a universal chime crying for the time
For forgiving.

There are those who find deep within their hearts
A rose bud opening and that's just the start.
We're brothers and sisters and we all are one.
If you find you're reaching for the gun
Hold your hands up for peace
Reach for the sun. Reach for the sun.

PART 1

The fifth petal is the petal of forgiveness. *And forgive us our trespasses as we forgive those who trespass against us.* This really brings us to the crux of the matter for, I believe, forgiveness lies at the heart of our healing journey. It feels such a huge process that I am caught between sensing I'm going to say too much whilst at the same time wanting to say nothing, for it is in the silence that we receive the answers we need. Unfortunately, for many, the story has become highly complex and confused. Much of the time perspectives get forgotten or so distorted that all that comes out of the silence is anger.

Like the prince in the *Sleeping Beauty* story, I want to cut away the brambles that have grown between ourselves and our truth to reveal that beauty that lies within the heart of us all. When we can truly see that, it becomes far more easy to forgive.

At the entrance of this petal, I was amazed at how thick my metaphorical bramble bushes still were. After years of processing and healing I naively thought I had cleared the way. It was obviously time to reach for my sword once more. My willingness to act on this meant it was easy to hack my way through, however, I could feel the thorns in my side as a reminder of the work yet to be done. Once inside, this terrain looked and felt different. My ability to immerse in the blessings of the natural world in all the past petals had now vanished.

This space felt empty, void of life, as if it had not been visited for centuries. The walls were dry and dusty, not even a weed growing up between the cracks. I shuddered not from the cold but the absence of warmth.

At the risk of sounding repetitive, I arrive hoping to investigate what has happened to our understanding of forgiveness as a culture. Again I feel that as we have continued to use our microscope rather than the telescope our view has lost its holistic perspective. It has become small-minded, proud and punitive. When the ego takes things personally, everything becomes a battle and empathy goes out the window.

I truly believe Deepak Chopra's words when he says that 'everyone is doing the best they can, given the limits of their consciousness.' I don't believe in Original Sin, or that people are naturally bad. I believe circumstances shut us down and make us behave in ways that simply act out our pain on others. Who can honestly say they behave impeccably at all times? When we recognise this maybe we would do well to look to our own behaviour before admonishing others.

A deed is often a two-way concern with a level of forgiveness needed on both sides. Sadly, we sometimes struggle more with forgiving ourselves than the 'other' but project our anger onto the other as a way of ignoring the main issue. Forgiving ourselves lies at the heart of everything, but knowing that there is anything to forgive is mostly hidden from our awareness. We cannot know what we don't know.

I sense my Minotaur, hiding in the dark recesses of this petal. The small amount of healing I experienced in the last petal was draining away through the cracks in the stone floor. A quick change in the light, like a flick of the tail, let me know of its presence but I would need more than that for any healing to take place here. I would have to see its face again. Did I want to?

I hold on to my positive thoughts. My conscious mind would have to dig deep to have any effect on the vast subterranean underbelly of my subconscious. I was discovering that Original Sin didn't come from the Jewish teaching, but I believed the seed was sewn there and that it lay at the heart of our feelings of disconnection. I spoke into the emptiness still holding the memory of my Minotaur's terrible face, hoping it would acknowledge my words as a mantra.

'It is my deepest wish to reinstate a level of compassion in people at all times, for kindness and empathy to become a natural thing in our society. I dream that the human psyche will emulate and nurture the healing vine rather than the thorny bramble to grow a more understanding and forgiving society.'

* * *

Up until this point, my life in Frome had brought me to such a busy state of being that the silence I craved, and had in abundance in my previous village life, had completely left me. It had been replaced by an overload of activity in both mind and body.

I had reached a crisis point in my body with my inch and a quarter pelvic twist. I was ready to stop and listen once more. As soon as I did this the answers started to flood in.

It was during these early spring months in 2015 that I had received some emails through a Jewish friend in Frome. It was an invitation to a walk that was 'Honouring Esther'. Esther was a Holocaust survivor who, towards the end of the war, had been forced to walk from a slave labour camp to a concentration camp as the Germans were retreating.

It was an arduous journey that would cost a great number their lives as so many were already frail and dangerously ill. Esther, however, survived this ordeal. She spent the next fifty years of her life telling her story. Her daughter was now choosing to pick up where Esther left off, continuing the healing work.

The 'forced walk', as her daughter explained, was to commemorate not only her mother's journey but also all those, from refugees to prisoners of war who have and continue to endure similar ordeals over the years. As we look back at the many terrible wars that followed the war that was meant to end all wars, the irony sits heavy on our shoulders.

Esther's daughter, Lorna, and her partner, who live in Bath, chose a walk that closely mirrored the shape of the path that her mother took in Germany. This two-day journey started in Frome and ended at the Jewish cemetery in Bath.

As I read the invitation I knew I wanted to connect in some way but knew that my asthma and back issues would prevent me from participating in the whole event. I wrote to the couple and asked if I could join them as they left Frome for the first hour or so and then leave them to it.

They graciously accepted my offer and as the April date approached my back felt strong enough and my asthma under control. Everything felt perfectly in place.

Although this was a big story, personally it was one I believed I had covered. I had forgiven Hitler, I had reconciled the war in my mind and believed that Hitler was mirroring the energy of the times. He was simply the personification of a hatred that had been boiling up since the injustices of the First World War that were the result of injustices of the past and so on. When the man on the street in Frome told me he wished Hitler had finished the job the first time I told my mum I didn't take it personally.

She replied, 'How could you not take it personally?'

I answered with a story much like Jo Berry's when she met the man who killed her father in the Brighton bombing. She said if they had sat down and had tea together they would have realised they were both decent human beings. It's only the dehumanising and 'othering' that we create in our minds that allows us to hate without any rationale.

Why else would some people really believe, what I thought was an inconceivable idea, that Jews have horns?

On the morning of the walk, a group of about twenty gathered in the centre of Frome. With the local press present, the town mayor and other interested parties, some words were spoken to send us on our way.

The structure for the walk was created by placing the maps of the two walks on top of each other and when the lines crossed the couple planned a stop and a chance to talk. They had recordings of Esther's public speeches which they played and a rich variety of offerings which they hoped would inspire discussion, poetry, photography and anything else that might come from the experience.

I ended up walking with them for about two hours which included three stops. The last stop was near Orchardleigh Estate, a beautiful country stately home, and already it felt as if we were in deep countryside. As the discussions began about the wartime experience, suddenly we heard a siren which was soon followed by sounds of explosions. For a moment everyone felt transported back in time.

Anyone who lives in Frome knows that we are situated near a quarry and on a quiet day when the wind is in the right direction, these warning sounds of a working quarry can be heard. They are neither frequent nor rare, however, it still didn't stop us thinking how perfectly timed it was as we were all totally immersed in the energy of this Second World War re-enactment.

It was the stop before that gave me the answer to a question I didn't even know I was asking. As we gathered, in the middle of a field I knew well, one on the edge of town, they played a recording of one of Esther's speeches. She told her story and although it was heartbreaking I can't remember anything she said. What followed, I remember clearly.

When the recording came to an end Esther's daughter, Lorna, began to talk of her life, growing up as the daughter of a Holocaust survivor. She spoke of the pain she suffered through her mother's trauma, and the tears began to stream down my face. I immediately questioned what was going on here. How was it that I could listen to the story of someone who had experienced extreme trauma and not be touched emotionally and yet be deeply moved by the daughter's?

Then it came to me, words that I had not spoken for thirty years, 'Oh I've seen it all before,' that I had uttered in the Holocaust museum in Israel flooded into my memory. Like a mist rising, in the clarity of the moment I saw how I had a huge capacity to release and cry over situations I felt I could handle, but, certain things, I had placed behind a great wall, a wall I didn't feel I could bear to look behind.

Although now, as an adult I felt I could deal with it, I believe I had kept this pain locked away since I was six years old when I first saw the sadness in my rabbi's eyes and was told of his life. Being far too young to understand or deal with such a story, locking it away was all my young mind could do and once it was there, out of sight at the heart of my labyrinth – and the labyrinth of my heart – it would be easy to forget there was a wall let alone something lurking behind there to be dealt with.

This is, I believe, the issue at the core of our collective trauma; the fact that we have no idea that we have anything to deal with either at a personal or cultural level. We have removed first the Minotaur, the shadow and then the labyrinth. Taking away this idea of journeying, we have lost the tools and indeed any sense of needing to do any work at all. So we roam the world, like spiritual children, with no knowledge of the pain we carry and no understanding of why we recreate this pain with such emotional devastation in our lives. It is time for us to face our inner truths and do the work; it is time for us to grow up.

My Minotaur is listening from the shadows.

* * *

The tears I shed for this wonderful woman who was working through her mother's pain was teaching me and helping me to bring down the walls that were concealing my own ancestral pain.

I returned home and told Mark of my experience and he was genuinely happy to help me in any way. He made many suggestions including taking a trip to Auschwitz. I thanked him but I knew that a trip into the labyrinth would be a better place to start, maybe less overwhelming.

So I meditated on the situation and I felt my Minotaur enter the space. I had been aware of its absence and almost glad of its return.

I take a deep breath, 'I want to thank you in advance of whatever we uncover here. I'm a little scared, but that's OK, I think.'

It says nothing but I can feel in my body a change, a warmth, only slight, but it is detectable. I now believed I had metaphorically peeked around the wall, and I sensed an answer would be easily found.

I knew that the Holocaust was not my personal story, and at the time I didn't even believe it was my ancestral story. (It was an investigation into Family Constellations that opened the door on the story of my grandfather's siblings who remained in Romania.)

My direct lineage, however, was the story of the Pogroms three or even four generations before me, but there was no one in living history to speak of what happened.

I went back to my altar and my meditation to ask what I should do. I remembered the intensity of the sob that had come through before and how I had decided to park it at that time. It was clearly time to return, the energetic thorns in my side tweaking at my skin like acupuncture needles.

The pain and the answers were hidden in my family story but until now it had always seemed like a closed book. This could be the gift.

I asked for the book to be opened and an answer came like a genie from a bottle. The words, 'Put the cross down,' clearly popped into my head.

As I considered the concept I remembered how we are being asked to bring Heaven to Earth, to remember the joy and not get caught up in the stories that bring us pain. It seemed as though I was holding layer upon layer of history. Just knowing that all I had to do was put it down, that the story was not mine but my ancestors', gave me such a sense of release I understood it immediately.

I felt hugely grateful. Suddenly I wanted to look my Minotaur in the face and laugh. But something didn't feel right, where was the sweat and tears? To let go of generations of pain couldn't be that easy. As my Minotaur turned and slunk back into the shadows, I knew soon enough I'd simply return to state and take up the cross again.

* * *

By this time the Palestinian theatre company, the Freedom Theatre would be arriving in the UK in just a few months and we, as a group, were on track for raising enough money to host them here in Frome. The jobs that had been assigned to me and another volunteer was to help design, set and print the theatre programme. I had the personal job of trying to sell advertising space in the programme to our local retailers. This was quite difficult as it was a one-off event and quite a niche subject. A real-life story based on a siege in Palestine in 2002 is not going to bring in the hordes. However, there were a few politically minded and sympathetic shop owners in our town and to them I am entirely grateful.

As the programme was getting close to being finalised certain shops were struggling to meet my deadline. Uncomfortable as I was, in this new role as fundraiser, I worried that my frequent 'I'm just popping in to check ...' was getting a little tiresome.

Then there was the payment. It was one thing agreeing to sell the advertising space but then I was having to collect the monies as well. This was a timely gift for me to work through my own relationship with money within my community. Of course, I did not have any problems, but I was grateful to be amongst people I knew, and who knew me well enough to joke about it. Here I was, a Jew selling advertising to fund a Palestinian theatre company to come to a Christian country; a complex issue for sure. A Holy Trinity?

It is often the way that when some guidance has been given, it is quickly followed by a test. I was being asked to let go of the story of my past and I was questioning whether I'd done the necessary work.

Only a day or so after receiving the guidance, I had to visit Hayley who had agreed to buy some advertising. She was the owner of a vintage shop called Lark. It was laid out on three floors; the ground floor brimming with beautiful old clothing and the other floors with interesting old furniture and artefacts, haberdashery and kitchenware from the years going back to before the war. The elegant rooms took you through the decades bringing back memories of childhood and beyond.

This time, we were hoping to complete the whole transaction but before we could get down to business, a couple walked in.

I stepped aside and the man asked Hayley about a plaster cross she had for sale, though I wasn't sure if I had heard this right. He started haggling on the price and when they were both happy he climbed the stairs to retrieve it.

While we waited I made polite conversation and asked his partner about the purchase. It seemed she didn't really share his excitement for it, especially when it was apparent that it was going to be hung in their kitchen.

Not really taking in what he was buying or what to expect, as he came down the stairs, very slowly, all was revealed. It was not just a cross but a five-foot, beautifully carved crucifix. It was quite badly damaged around his legs but that didn't put the man off. However beautiful, I had to admit, it wouldn't be the kind of thing I would choose to have in my kitchen.

It obviously weighed quite a lot and Hayley indicated that he could put it on the sofa that was conveniently in the shop. As he carefully laid it down, the words, 'Put the cross down,' came back to me and I had to stifle my giggles. Just in case I'd let myself get distracted from my purpose, here it was being pushed under my nose.

I didn't know Hayley that well, so I didn't say anything, I

just concluded my business with her after the couple and their purchase had left. It was a while before I realised I wanted to use this story and should ask her permission before mentioning her and her shop. Although I was a little nervous about asking her, she was, as I'd hoped, very excited about the whole story.

'You know me, Vicki, I love that kind of thing too.'

I somehow knew it wouldn't have happened in anyone else's shop.

* * *

So, easy, just live the joy. The message was clear, the pain isn't mine, just put it down. But something was missing. Although my back was better, the asthma was still there and so was the mountain range of bound muscle in the small of my back and my arse. Somehow I still felt I was just scraping the surface.

I took to my meditation mat once more and asked what I should do with this. I stepped back into the story with my grandma and the negative energy I believed she had handed down to me through my mum.

As I flipped through the slides of my memory, as though leafing through a filing cabinet, once again I felt my Minotaur's presence. Now it felt as if it was breathing down my neck. I shuddered.

'What have you found?' Its voice was low and calm.

'Am I getting warm?' I asked flippantly. There was no response, so I started talking just to fill the silence. 'A few years back I had realised that I hadn't fully thanked my grandma for the gift of my house, being as I was, too wrapped up in guilt and worry that she wouldn't approve of how I was living my life, now I could live mortgage free.

'In 2010 when I was told about the links with the maternal line and asthma, I believed I understood the whole story and put that to rights. With that cleared and gratitude fully offered, looking back, I realised that this was actually only half the story. Now I needed to forgive her for all the pain I believe she's inflicted on my mother.'

My Minotaur stepped in to help, 'Can you see how you only connect with your mind. You've been completely ignoring your body all this time.' It spoke in a matter of fact tone but I sensed there were layers going back millennia.

'Yes, I know that now, it's badly in need of addressing. Any tips?' I held up my hands and felt the energy slip down my into my body. 'I can do this,' I said reassuringly. 'I can forgive my grandma.' I was feeling magnanimous.

This felt really important, like it was something, a moment in my life that I was always destined to reach. I wanted to sense my spiritual guides applauding me, a huge mission completed. But there was nothing.

And then it hit me, like a smack around the head. For at least ten years I had been working with forgiveness, writing songs, a book and my play was meant to hit it right on the nail. Had I still not got it?

I can't remember exactly how it was conveyed to me but suddenly it dawned on me that I was the one doing the judging here. The teaching that I was trying to put out into the world with my work, that everyone is doing the best they can with the tools that they have, is a philosophy I have tried to live by in every moment. It was being brought to my attention that I had forgotten these words when it came to my own grandma.

I sensed my Minotaur settle in, like any teacher who wants to be there when a pupil is reaching for attainment. I continued,

'Funny, that we can be so good at helping other people see the light when it comes to judgement or forgiveness but it when it comes to dealing with issues ourselves we can become very selective or even blind.' I knew it was agreeing with me.

So, here I was being my grandmother's grandchild, passing the intolerance back up to her. I was being pulled up sharply and gently rapped over the knuckles, by myself, of course. I was judging my own grandmother with little or no knowledge of what she had been through in her life, what traumas she, and those before her, had experienced. I was blaming her for having lost one of the most basic instincts a mother has for her children; to demonstrate love.

I metaphorically bowed my head. I had been judging her for the last fifty years and I deeply hoped she would forgive me. I knew as it was asked, it was done.

It was like a huge weight was lifted from me. That cross that I'd been carrying around with me was not the one I thought I shouldered. It bore a different hue and taste but I truly felt I had cleared it now.

I wait, hanging out for a response. My Minotaur has not moved but a faint glow emanates from the space around it and its shadow pales.

I begin to feel movement like the earth stirring beneath me and I sense a vibration, of life returning. The healing vines are beginning to wind their way up through the cracks in the stone floor where the brambles once held vigil. In my mind I sense the hall of mirrors, the ancestral echoes of my life path, are being uncovered, the obstructions being released and the energy starting to flow like an unblocked spring.

I do a quick internal survey, checking for an ability to breathe more easily; but get no positive response. I'm still not home yet.

*   *   *

I thought that maybe it was time to broach the subject of my play with my parents, so one day I just dropped it into the conversation again. It began with a discussion about the Middle East. Then a week or so later we had another. They were fairly heated as I now had a whole new understanding of the situation and many first-hand stories from people who have worked as EAPPIs (Ecumenical Accompaniment Programme in Palestine and Israel), people who are willing to stand at the border in the West Bank witnessing what is happening there. 'It can be a pretty traumatising undertaking.' The words just come out.

'And how did that go down?' My Minotaur emerges.

I relax a little. 'You see, it's tricky,' I reflected, 'my parents are very aware of how badly the Israeli government is behaving and are really unhappy about that. But they are also very aware of how the Israelis have been treated over the last few decades. This is the problem, no one's hands are clean.'

'So …?'

'Well, it just so happened, help was at hand.'

'More divine intervention?'

'You could call it that. I had attended a few meetings, set up by a newcomer to Frome who is a university lecturer and a Fellow in Reconciliation, where we discussed the nature of discussion. The evenings were challenging on many levels and I frequently fell into the trap as my heartbeat increased, my cheeks flushed as my ego felt threatened. After three sessions I had arrived at a place where, when I remembered, I could notice my ego jumping into reaction and so temper it. The timing couldn't have been more perfect.'

I recalled the conversation with my parents, aware that I

could only report from my point of view. 'I think what happened was, the next time the discussion came up, I reached a place when I realised I no longer could hold my own with the facts. As this was never my strength, I stepped aside and let them let off some steam. It was then I could gather myself, calm my heartbeat and my need for approval and explain how actually I believed that finding a way to peace, like in the story of *Romeo and Juliet*, will only happen when someone decides enough is enough. When so much blood has been shed and no one can remember how it all began, what does it take for someone to choose to put down their gun and offer the other a cup of coffee instead?'

'And did that work?'

I sighed, 'it was like a balloon had burst. All the energy went out the room and my dad said, "Is that what your play is about?"'

I am still only beginning to understand the magnitude of the process that I went through with my parents. It feels remarkable and is still unfolding.

My work with Family Constellations that I ventured into a few years later told me that its main purpose is to allow the love to come through from our ancestors. When we remove the blocks then we can ultimately make peace with our parents. I had very little conflict with mine but it seemed like I had pushed through all the barriers to find the most tricky in our relationship to overcome.

I do wish to honour them both here as I am very aware that few people would be open-minded enough to arrive at this place of peace with their daughter over such a contentious issue. But I know I wouldn't have even broached the subject had I not thought they were able to meet me in the middle. I am very blessed.

So the next day I sent my play to them. By this time I had read it to many people and done quite a lot of tweaks and edits and now felt it was ready to be staged. I had gathered a few willing actors to help me stage it as a script-in-hand rehearsed reading. It just so happened that four generous actors were willing to give me some of their time and were coming over the following day to read it through.

That next afternoon, I was very surprised when I spoke to my parents and they told me they had already read it. I gathered myself for their comments and they told me that they had thoroughly enjoyed it. Then my mother started to tell me that though she thought it was very dramatic and emotional, she didn't really get the ending. As I tried to offer an explanation, she kept talking about the moment at the end of the first half. Eventually it dawned on me that she had obviously not read any further. My parents are pretty good with computers and downloading documents but something had clearly gone amiss. No wonder she didn't get the ending.

With promises that they'd get back to it and read the rest, I suddenly became a little nervous. The first half is really quite tame and is just about setting the background to what needs to happen to reach a point of breakdown so the healing can come through.

I realise my Minotaur is quietly laughing at me.

'You might well think it's funny, and what was worse, that evening when the actors turned up on my doorstep, I had my first taste of having the play read to me, to receive it. Up until now, I had only read it to people, which is a completely different experience.'

I remember sitting there as the second half was played out, shrinking into my seat. The actors were excellent in bringing the characters to life. I just had to remind myself to breathe.

I tried to hear it as my parents might and I began to worry. Would they be as gracious about the second, more hard-hitting, part of the play, where one of the characters struggles to reconcile the universal story, the idea that his enemy is really his brother, or even himself?

The next day there was silence, and the next.

I was determined not lose my nerve so I waited. But I couldn't help worrying that I had pushed the limit of their tolerance too far and that they simply didn't know how to respond. I didn't want to call to ask them, as I was struggling with what I might hear if I did, so I waited. Only four days had passed but it seemed like so much longer.

When I finally found some other minor reason to pick up the phone, I was able to casually drop in, 'So did you read the rest of my play then?' I wasn't sure if I hadn't just dropped a live hand grenade or not. I held my breath and waited for the answer.

'Oh yes,' my dad equally casually replied. 'We enjoyed it very much, I thought you dealt with the story in a really even-handed way.'

'Really?!' I said. The relief was immense.

On reflection I felt that even if they hadn't enjoyed the play, we would have been able to find a place of peace. On a subject so overflowing with emotive feelings and conflict it was an important thing we achieved. At this moment I wasn't aware how important the timing of this resolution had been.

PART 2

I have long held the view, put forward by Gandhi, that whatever change you want to see in the world you have to start with yourself, and I sense that to do this fully I need to take into consideration everything about myself, my whole lineage.

Because I often get caught up in overcomplicating things I have become a great believer in using images. I think they can say so much and often can reduce a complex idea into a state of simplicity with one swipe. The big-picture cartoon version is something I have grown to love, and when they arrive in my mind it seems to me like my guides are trying to stop me from over philosophising, from muddying the waters. Humour, also, wins hands down every time.

Around this time one particular image started to seep into my mind. It was an acrobatic act, rather like Jacob's ladder, with a person at the bottom and all the ancestors on their shoulders, starting with the parents and then the grandparents and on and on, back up into the sky. It was like a scene out of a Buster Keaton movie. I saw them at the bottom, maybe on a unicycle to add to the comedy, scampering around trying to keep the ladder steady as the ladder begins to look like an ever-widening snake.

The image is a jolly one, as my guides always communicate with joy and, of course, the love is falling down the ladder from on high. However, it is also painfully clear that alongside the love, we also carry the burdens that the past generations have not dealt with.

The ladder becomes so huge that the structure disappears into the clouds. I keep this image to mind when I am attempting to put my house in order.

I had been living in a permanent state of judgement with my grandmother all my life, opening this door started to ignite my memory, helping me to make sense of it all.

* * *

In order to access the necessary doors to this closed mindset we have embraced for so long, my mind took me back to a gig in Bristol. My Minotaur is moving around and so I wait for it to settle, I know it wants to hear and I feel I can now recognise when it's going to appear.

'You think you've got me sussed?' It whispers, like it's just behind my ear.

I try not to jump. 'I think so, I'm beginning to understand my own stuff better so it's only natural that would reflect on you.'

'Accepted.' It pulls back, creating a little more distance, far more comfortable, I feel. I bring my thoughts back to the gig.

'After I had finished performing my songs, the venue was in a cafe, a few of us gathered in the front bar to have a drink. We were just chatting happily, but quite intensely, until a woman started talking about her anger towards the men in her life and men in general. I felt very strongly that this issue is core to many of our problems in society. I found I couldn't keep quiet.'

'Did you get on your high horse?' My Minotaur drops it in effectively.

'Maybe? I have been asked to get off my soap box before, or maybe I'm just blowing my bugle? It's a fine line isn't it, one I've always struggled to balance.'

'Just remember, people can only respond from their own perspective on life.'

I let that settle. I'd have to find a quiet moment to dwell on that truth.

'For me,' picking up where I'd left off, 'it goes back to being stuck in judgement, just outside the gates of the Garden of Eden, our left brain fighting against our right, Cain killing Abel. As we create this battle between the masculine and feminine aspects of ourselves into our world around us, it manifests itself as the battle of the sexes we experience today. It's the oldest story in the oldest book in our culture.'

'And how does this relate to your story?'

'I suggested to the woman that this blanket judgement of men really doesn't help and that perhaps some forgiveness was needed.'

'And how did that go down?' My Minotaur wasn't mocking me but neither was it expecting a good response.

'Well, as you can imagine, not too well, especially when I tried to explain that maybe anger wasn't helpful here either.'

'Oooh.'

'OK, I know, from one who always suppresses emotions I have a lot to learn when it comes to handling other's!' I'm beginning to lose my confidence here.

'And what did she reply?'

'She told me, and of course she was right, that I was judging her for being angry, and that she had every right to be.'

'Indeed.'

'So, having lost my ability to think on my feet like I used to, I replied, "Yes, of course you have the right to be angry. I apologise, I have no right to judge you."'

'But you're always saying, if anything, you think too much.' My Minotaur is mocking me now.

'Yes, but I make things too complicated, trying to see the whole picture all the time. I get caught up multiple avenues of thought. Choosing the right one takes time, it's a process that needs to be slept on. I couldn't find a good response in the moment, so I let the subject drop.'

The next morning I awoke with the whole conversation resounding in my brain. Now it was obvious. What I had wanted to say, but didn't have the presence of mind, was that, of course, she has the right to be angry. But who wants to live with that anger? While there is nothing wrong with anger in itself, if it's not worked through in a healthy way, it can either turn into violent action or fester inside us. If it is not released then it can be incredibly damaging to your whole mind, body and spirit, bringing about feelings of dis-ease. I was dismayed that I couldn't bring this idea to her as a gentler way of living in the world, a way that was kinder to herself. However, I also needed to recognise that we can only be brought to this idea when we are ready; once again timing being everything.

I was beginning to understand that people believe that when they forgive someone they are somehow 'letting them off the hook', absolving them of their crime. I don't believe this is the case. Forgiveness is not about saying that what the person did was OK. Whatever has happened cannot be undone, how we deal with internally it is what matters.

*   *   *

Sometimes we get so caught up in the pain and injustice of what has happened to us, it gives us a sense of identity which is often hard to let go of. It seemed incredibly important to understand this idea of identity a little better. How else can we make sense of the forgiveness that is so needed, especially as the healing can only start when we recognise that the conflict also lies within.

When I moved to Frome I was becoming increasingly interested in my DNA. I kept talking about my Russian, Romanian and Polish blood but then I started to question, if we we're only there a few hundred years, what it takes to belong to the land. Is it simply by eating the food, knowing that we are what we eat? I suggested to my mum the idea that we must have married out at some point during 'the good times'? She responded by saying if we were still here as part of the Jewish clan then no, if we'd married out we would not have been able to stay in the community.

It was at this time that, discovering that Frome had one of the three DNA test centres in the UK, (I had stopped being surprised by what Frome consistently had to offer) I sent off for my results. I was amazed. My top four places of origin were Yemen, Saudi Arabia, Iraq and Ethiopia. Any European blood didn't feature more than 5 per cent. Even my recent history which is just the past ten generations was only 50 per cent East and Southern Europe, the rest being the Near East. My white face, but obvious Middle Eastern features, was something I had just accepted but not fully analysed before.

The Jewish journey, to peel back the layers and see that we were Arabs before we were Jews and that we were also once pagans, (which is true of everyone) was revealing a conflict I needed to resolve. How could I reconcile and shift the emotions of centuries of trauma while understanding that we have, in recent times, obtained power and abused it with the shift in our skin colour? We are hated for the ancient conflict created by not accepting Christ and in modern times, for becoming powerful and wealthy despite or even as a result of the oppression and impoverishment the Dispersion brought. And then there's Israel.

I wanted to stop, be the witness and choose another path. However, I knew this would upset the status quo. If I denounced those who allow the suffering to be considered simply as 'what we have to do to keep ourselves safe' I would be called a self-hating Jew or even a traitor. Yet to me, donning the white face of supremacy is creating a false identity, a false sense of power over our brothers and sisters.

Personally, I couldn't see how we were showing up as a 'Light unto the Nations'?

My mission was to heal my inner conflict around this, even though to travel on that road would draw criticism from many quarters. I needed to look elsewhere for instruction, to find ways that were steeped in kindness and empathy.

Indigenous people say that the land is our healer and teacher. I knew that as a displaced Jew I had lost my connection and the ability to listen to its wisdom. How to return to a place of being in right relation to it would be the imperative.

I know the three Abrahamic religions each offer great wisdom, holding the original essence of divinity and beauty at their core. Over the centuries, there have been translations and interpretations bringing conflict after conflict. We have brought these deep wounds with us to this broken state.

The Jewish story of coming full circle, of losing our sense of belonging and now returning home – a home gifted by the post-Holocaust guilt-ridden West – with that loss at the heart of our being, we have now subconsciously chosen to become the oppressors thinking this is what is necessary in order to survive. Something seems to have gone awry with our story of *The Alchemist*.

I sense my Minotaur is leaning in as I start stepping into dangerous territory.

'It feels important to understand this, to unpick the story without blame or judgement, just as I did with my grandma, to truly feel and release the pain. If we don't do this work then it appears in dark and incomprehensible ways.'

My Minotaur remains silent.

* * *

We have seen judgement and polarisation in the UK become such a thing in our times, that the need to demonise those who we disagree with has created great distortions in our ideals. In-fighting has ripped both the main political parties in two. The tabloid media, with its constant need to sensationalise, has amplified this through its monopolised power base.

While I watch the Conservative Party continue to wreak havoc in this country, I'm still trying to understand how the Labour Party has lost so much ground, a party that always prided itself on being excepting of all races and religions with strong ethical foundations.

The internal political battles and clamours for righteousness continue to become distorted. The belief that socialism was born out of the need to look after the community rather than the individual and in particular the underdog, brings this all closer to home; another of our shadows we struggle to look in the eye.

I hear the war cries, the interpretations of the calls against Zionist aggression being renamed as antisemitism. This has blurred the distinction between Jews and Israelis and their government. This is even more pertinent when I contemplate the idea that the story of Jerusalem, as the spiritual heart of our culture, like the symbolic Russian dolls, mirrors all our stories.

'How can we find clarity here?' I ask rhetorically.

My Minotaur tries to bring me back to a rational place. 'Knowing your history, the full story, is what's crucial here. When fingers are pointed at those who point fingers, we have to make sure we have done our homework. Otherwise ignorance means people can easily be led astray. We have to listen to both sides.'

'And then we have to be prepared to forgive?'

My Minotaur responds with a silence that I recognise; an acknowledgement.

My natural response is to tell a story.

I saw a beautiful online video of an old Jewish lady who was a victim of Dr Mengele in the Second World War. It took her until very recently, to reach a place when she was ready to forgive him for the pain he inflicted on herself and her twin sister, who died at his hand. The moment she did this, she felt free. She explained that for the first time in her eighty years she felt empowered because she had released herself from this lifelong experience of pain she had been holding on to. What saddened me was the amount of abuse she received for simply writing a letter to the dead man; from those who couldn't open their hearts to an old woman who chose to be free of her lifelong pain.

This is the *Romeo and Juliet* story that we know so well. It has been written many times, and is imbedded in our psyche but has somehow been ignored, put in the box marked 'idealistic'.

When I finished writing my song *Sulha* a tragic story hit our news of another racial attack. The mother of the murdered boy stood on television and said, 'Forgive them, they know not what they do.'

I knew these words, but hearing them in a real context, back in 2005, this rang bells of joy in my heart. My response was to write the song *Forgiving* and dedicate it to the Walker family.

Our inner conflict, born of the teaching of Original Sin that we are constantly playing out on the 'other' in our world, is a truth that I believe no longer serves us. The G-d that for eons we knew to simply be 'good' or love, that was a part of us in every sense of the word, has been ripped from our hearts. It feels as if, since our eviction from the Garden of Eden we are told that we are to blame.

We have subliminally consented to this judgement because of the stories we have been told. Few are taught about dissenting

Lilith, but we all know about the subordinate, consenting Eve whose actions, so we are taught, cast us out of our home. She is blamed for the pain we have suffered since; Cain killing Abel, our heads being cut off from our hearts which has allowed us to kill our fellow humans in the name of G-d and slowly destroy our environment and our ability to thrive.

The story we have created of being cast out of our home, is something I continually question, sensing it is a perspective that has hidden the real truth from us; that we never left G-d and G-d never left us.

This journey is just a part of the whole experience of being human, the in and out breath, a movement towards and away from G-d. We are travelling on a vast Galactic Cycle that the Mayans and other indigenous people – who still live connected to these Universe truths – have never forgotten.

Through the millennia, the loss of this wisdom has created irreconcilable rifts between families, lovers, nations and religions. The Abrahamic religions have been taken and manipulated to such a degree that there are many set against each other with an inability to forgive at a core level.

I believe we can choose differently.

*   *   *

Forgiveness and reconciliation are processes I always respond to in an emotional way. I studied *Romeo and Juliet* for O level and I always loved Bernstein's *West Side Story*, its twentieth-century rendition. (At school, I even put on a classroom version of *Romanoff and Juliet*, Peter Ustinov's interpretation of the story.)

I remember, soon after arriving in my house in Frome, the song *Somewhere*, from *West Side Story*, kept coming into my awareness, bringing a lump to my throat and a tear to my eye. Something was forming in my mind without my conscious knowledge of it.

The film, *The Railway Man* came out around this time, and when the reconciliation came and the credits started to roll, I couldn't move from my seat; I could only sob, moved by the beauty of the resolution of years of pain.

We are living in a state of amnesia, having used our emotional intelligence to shut down the parts unable to deal with the pain of the original conflict. How much are we prepared to endure and how much longer can we live with generations of tombstones all piling up on top of each other.

If someone is brave enough to put down their sword or gun – and we have seen this in some of the most hardened gangs in America – and the other responds, the ripple effect is immeasurable. We all grow. This is what so excited me when my father really got when I was trying to explain what my play was about.

By the time I wrote my play I had already decided that I wanted the song *Somewhere* to be the finale, to have it played when they all sat down to drink the third and final cup of coffee. I even worked it out on the harp.

When I was underway with finding actors for my play in early 2015 I began organising the music. I had my two peace songs, *Sulha* and *Forgiving*, now I just had to sort the third.

To get permission to perform this seminal song I got in touch with the copyright holders and received an immediate response.

'First,' the man said, 'can I thank you for getting in touch and asking for permission. So many people really don't bother. However,' he went on very apologetically, 'I'm afraid I can't give you permission in this instance.'

'Oh,' I said. I discovered that permission is rarely given if you are taking something and putting it in an entirely different context. So I decided to put the idea on hold with the plan of 'sleeping on it'. This was my usual tried and tested way of dealing with brick walls.

That evening Jo Berry took me to Bristol to see the film that she was featured in called *Beyond Right and Wrong*, the title inspired by the Rumi poem. The inner city community centre, where it was showing, was not far from my parents. I knew the centre well and as we took the lift to the third floor, it was not only our physical selves that were being elevated. It was incredibly moving and her story was just one of five including others from Rwanda and Israel.

I realised, with all the busyness of Frome, working on my book and writing plays, I hadn't written a song for over a year. However, now I had a need, a subject matter and some inspiration. 'I should write one myself,' I thought.

This wasn't my first introduction to Rumi, a Sufi poet from the thirteenth century, but this poem kept flying around my head. I sat at my harp and wrote my song *I'll Meet You There*. It is a fusion of his words with some additional ones of mine (I can only hope he is OK with this collaboration) and my music. The composition happened with such flow, no rocks or mental boulders. I felt the love pour through it. I used the template of Bernstein's song as a starting point and then let it develop. An interesting characteristic is that it is a minor song that goes to the major at the end; from melancholic to joyful. It is called a *tierce de Picardy* and Wikipedia describes it *'as a form of resolution'*. I love that.

* * *

May brought the Freedom Theatre, from Palestine to Frome. The Merlin Theatre was packed to the gills and it was a tremendous success. The FFoP, as is their wont, hosted the company beautifully, with good food, and accommodated them with people who understood their needs and language. We even organised a friendly football match with Frome's local team, aware that amongst the bigger day-to-day problems that the Palestinians face, sometimes it's the small things that matter, like having a game of football, knowing that so many of their pitches had been removed.

As Theatre Studies was one of my A level subjects, I was very excited to help the company with their 'get in' and see how their Church of the Nativity was built on the stage so simply but effectively. Then the show began.

I must admit, having put so much effort into the many months of planning their arrival, I hadn't really considered the impact the play itself would have on me. As it came to the close and the clever use of real news footage was screened on the outside of the church wall as they reluctantly gave up the long siege, it hit me. The realisation that all that had been played out for us was a recounting of real events and that although the actors weren't part of this story, they lived with this kind of resistance against oppression daily. As everyone began applauding as the play came to an end, once again I could only sob.

I am constantly amazed by the different ways people are affected by stories, from those that are untouched to a watery, snotty mess, such as mine. I take on the pain of others, as well as the joy. This was still something I wasn't fully acknowledging in myself. It had been the end of a long journey for me, although another was just beginning, and there was much to cry about.

Two weeks later I was to put on my own play, kindly helped

by the FFoP. I also have to thank the Frome Drama Club and the members who worked with me to make this happen, particularly Laurie Parnell who took on many roles, finding the right actors, helping to organise rehearsals and taking one of the four challenging parts and portraying him exactly as I saw him.

I am very grateful to the few people who came to see it. The performance was a success and I really enjoyed the Q and A that followed. Many felt it was deeply transformative and wanted to be supportive of its next steps. This included Jo Berry who I felt honoured to have in the audience. One of the main energies behind the FFoP, Adam, who also felt moved by it, encouraged me when he said,

'I don't usually speak up at these events.' His energy was usually taken up doing most of the work behind the scenes, 'But for the first time I felt I was able to see the other side of the story.' This was coming from a man who had spent time with both Jews and Palestinians, and had a great deal of awareness of the whole issue.

I knew as it was gifted to me, it had worth and this gave me the courage of my conviction, after all there is a place 'beyond right and wrong.'

* * *

That summer, Rebecca, a new friend in Frome, wanted to introduce me to her other 'Jewish, asthmatic friend.' When I met Jo we did all have a good laugh about this, not the usual premise on which to introduce people, but Frome is anything but usual.

We decided to have a day out and Rebecca wanted to take us to a beach, to an area she loved on the south coast. It was August and luckily the sun was shining beautifully. My neighbour had the same idea, so we all took off to our separate but similar destinations.

We drove to the beach at Burton Bradstock and on the journey we chatted all the way. We soon discovered that although our age, culture and ailments were very much the same, how we got here could not have been more different. There was plenty to empathise over and plenty to laugh about.

By the time we parked a wind was whipping up. We grabbed a quick lunch and although the beach was lovely, because of the strong wind, I put in my plea for a change of scenery.

Rebecca suggested a visit to St Catherine's Chapel, situated nearby at a place called Abbotsbury. A little chime went through my heart as this name keeps coming up for me; a past life story associated with Catherine Parr, I had moved into Catherine Street in Frome and my play had just been put on in St Catharine's Parish Hall. I later learned she is, aptly, the patron of good marriage.

It didn't take long to get there and the weather continued to turn against us. As we walked up the steep incline to the chapel the light grew dimmer and I felt my heart beat a little quicker. The chapel is gutted with a long history but I entered with no knowledge, just an open mind. It wasn't long before we had the place to ourselves and we all instinctively started playing with the beautiful acoustics. I began to do some over-toning, creating harmonics with my voice and then Jo sang a song.

When she had finished, I overcame any initial feelings of self-consciousness and my new song for peace came into my mind. I started to sing.

'There's a field, beyond right and wrong,
Where there is peace and song,
I'll meet you there.'

Immediately a white dove flew in and rested on an alcove above my head. I stopped singing in astonishment and looked up. Overcome with a powerful sense of acknowledgement, the tears rolled down my cheek and we all held our breath. I wanted to get a better look so I moved to the other side of the chapel and continued with my song.

'There's a field, where the earth meets the sky,

Where you and I, can find love for free unconditionally.'

And another dove flew in and sat by its side.

'And we'll weep, until the rivers run deep,

As we cry, our healing hearts touch the sky.'

My tears continued to fall and we all were held in the reverence of the moment.

'There's a field, beyond right and wrong, where we all belong,

I'll meet you there.'

When I finished we remained suspended in the reverberations and then from the nest three little baby doves rose their heads and started tweeting for food. It was so beautiful, it felt like my prayer for peace had been heard.

It was time to leave. As we walked down the hill from the chapel in reverent silence, Rebecca stopped and looked back. The whole chapel was shrouded in mist.

'I just realised, that was my dream last night,' she said, 'it was exactly like this.' We all laughed. This wasn't the first time Rebecca had had these premonitions in her dreams. However, when I got home and bumped into my neighbours I discovered that they had only been 20 miles away from us, but had perfect sunshine all day.

* * *

Reconciliation and forgiveness have become essential features in my life. As they weave their magic, helping me to find peace, they also push me further into the comfortable and the uncomfortable side of my relationship with myself, something I will never stop investigating.

I have come to understand that there are people who are afraid of conflict and people who fear working through conflict. There are those that suppress emotions and those who default into reactive emotions, such as fear or anger, as a means of avoidance. These are all different responses to pain we all hold. There are those that work out their pain on themselves and those that work out their pain on others; one being an explicit and the other an implicit reaction. Most of us, of course, go through life managing both ways of reacting, simultaneously.

If we recognised that we are all victims of this journey into separation, simply expressing our pain in different ways, maybe we would choose compassion rather than judgement as a standard response.

I am arriving at a place where I feel I have no choice but to acknowledge that this is a major aspect of our Minotaur. It seems to me that much of this came about as we began to reduce G-d to a quantifiable being, a being that has personality traits that we bestow on it, good or otherwise. We began to see G-d in our own collective image, not the other way round. The G-d we now revere and fear is just society pointing its fingers back at ourselves, like the Michelangelo painting of G-d and Adam. However, you cannot fit G-d within a frame, it is beyond judgement and limitation and beyond our understanding of love.

This is how I see we developed the Minotaur, the shadow aspect of our psyche. Spirituality was harnessed by the mind, like a lasso, and dragged out of the heart and bound into organised religions.

What was created, the Synagogue, the Church, the Mosque, grew out of the beauty of its origins, while dogma and corruption created the beast. Whatever you looked for, was reflected back as the beauty, the beast and everything in between. And so, through unresolved conflict, we have walked the journey of splitting apart until one way of being became many.

I came to learn that conflict is life, it is part of living in the physical world. How we deal with it is crucial. Conflict is good and healthy if it is discussed around the table. If it ends up in violence or division, then there is work to be done. If it is ignored, then our Minotaur has to wait for its time. Meanwhile it feeds on our fear and lack of engagement.

As I look around the country I see people in pain. Having set ourselves free of the ties of a religious path we have been cast adrift. Seeking a new anchor without good guidance, we have made bad choices and have now hooked onto new icons to revere.

One, the media, feeds us fear, keeps our lives on amber, or even red, alert and constantly shows us where to point the finger. It isn't easy to see the bigger picture when your life is threatened on all sides. This is what our government, media and commerce and, of course, we are all doing, to prevent ourselves from waking up and seeing the shadow for what it truly is. Also, it is important to remember, there is no 'them', only 'us'.

It is important to recognise that life is like a story, and in this episode, the one that we are all currently subscribing to, we have reached a relatively new consensus. What would it take to view things differently, step outside the box, if we chose to? For instance, the Internet can be seen as a beautiful interlocking web or a golden calf, either way it is simply mirroring our interconnectedness and it's up to us how we wield its magic.

The astrology is fascinating. Just for starters, in May 2018, Uranus, a revolutionary and explosive planetary energy, moved into Taurus. The last time Uranus, on its eighty-four year cycle, did this was in 1934. A few years ago, the political tide started turning and far right wing governments started coming to power in some European countries and Trump started making waves in the USA as did UKIP in the UK. There was a distinct feeling like we were returning to the pre-war times. This does not mean we are doomed to repeat our actions. It means we have the choice to repeat or to make a change. In every moment we are offered the chance to choose between the shadow or the light.

The way, I believe, we can work through conflict successfully is through forgiveness; forgiving ourselves so we can look at others as mirrors and begin to forgive them too. We can only do this when we learn to relax into our bodies and recognise that we hold both fear and love in our hearts. When we tip the balance towards compassion and empathy, we release the tension we bear and soften into a more gentle way of living.

The Minotaur defines the energy of our duality, being half-human, half-beast. It understands how to coexist in a state of polarity. Like the yin/yang symbol each holds the seed of the other in its heart. Neither the dark nor the light is good or bad, just opposites. The shadow is cast when we judge.

As I begin to understand how conflict can exist in a peaceful way, whether it is within myself, religion, politics, our institutions, between neighbours or neighbouring countries, I hope to come to a place where I can accept everyone for who they are without prejudgement. This is all part of the journey to forgiveness and it begins with ourselves. If we can learn to do this as a society we might stop trying to remove others from our lives and begin to live together in peace, for we all have our imperfections. When we can celebrate our differences life becomes an amazing journey.

CHAPTER SIX

THE SIXTH PETAL: STRENGTH

Lead us not into temptation but deliver us from evil.

I'll Meet You There

There's a field, beyond right and wrong
Where there is peace and song.
I'll meet you there.

There's a field, where the Earth meets the sky,
Where you and I can find love for free, unconditionally.

And we'll weep, until the rivers run deep.
As we cry, our healing hearts touch the sky.

There's a field, beyond right and wrong
Where we all belong.
I'll meet you there.

PART 1

The sixth petal is the petal of Strength. *Lead us not into temptation but deliver us from evil.* We have arrived at the final leg of this journey into the labyrinth. After the difficult middle section, when the end is so far in sight you feel homesick, now the finish is within reach, I sense it can still go any way. They say most car accidents happen when you are five minutes from home, when the tiredness pulls at your eyelids and you're so close the concentration lags. Other times a final spurt of energy can revitalise your whole system and you can feel yourself running for the finishing line.

I step into the new space and I feel a need to ground myself; completion is not an easy task.

The air in here is different again from the last petal and I watch, circumspect, for the first signs of life to grow up around the stonework. I see a little way off the grass is taking root in places but I have to be careful before getting ahead of myself. There is still much work to be done. The garden has to fully take shape in my mind and if I can visualise it and feel it, then my hope is that it can't be far off from becoming a reality. After all isn't that how we shape our world?

To do this I have to understand all aspects of this petal. While we have placed too much importance on our physical strength and ignored our inner, core strength, rediscovering what this really means will, I believe, guide us home back to the garden. When we examine the word evil, the negative aspects that we hope to avoid, like temptation, these words have become etched into our psyche. I have learned that the brain doesn't understand negatives. It is like telling a child, 'don't do that!' No sooner said, than done.

Evil, I believe, has been deeply misunderstood. 'To sin' actually just means to miss the mark; to stray from the path or act out of a lack of love. As we continue to lose our way, the hammer of judgement is something our culture is only too keen to wield, without stopping to understand what damage it can cause. I believe this comes from a feeling of powerlessness.

The Leo archetype holds the energy of our true power, found

in our Solar Plexus, our inner radiance. When this chakra is open it works having 'power with' others rather than wanting 'power over' others; the wounded masculine needing domination over the suppressed feminine. This wisdom, once it is rediscovered, rebalances us, and brings simplicity and peace into our lives. It removes competition and replaces it with cooperation, fear with love. It redefines and reinstates evil to simply being an absence of G-d, like dark is to light; all you need to do is to light a match.

Immediately a stream of light pours in from a dark recess of the petal.

'Where does that put me?' My Minotaur is here with me again, testing me.

'In what sense?' I ask, not wanting to second guess it.

My Minotaur moves a little nearer but still out of view. 'I am a creature, with the body of a human and the head and tail of a beast, half mythical, half of this world; half of the dark and half light. However, in our fervour to judge we have turned away from many truths and in our fear of what we don't understand we have tried to cut ourselves off from what we believe to be evil.'

I stand up with the intention of seeing it fully this time, but I hold back.

It continues, 'In fearing the opposite of what is light, as we cling to what we believe is "good", we misunderstand what lies in the darkness. We use the word shadow, but they are not the same thing; dark and shadow. Stepping into the dark side of ourselves does not make us evil. It is just the dualistic nature of our world.

'While on the path of separation we are invited to bring the duality into oneness, bring Heaven to Earth, manifest light out of the void. Of course, this journey is not necessarily an easy one, for the closer we get to the light the more it challenges us, revealing our equally powerfully dark side. This is the law of creation; reminding us that there is no good or bad, just opposites that need balancing, like electrical charges, positive and negative or receiving and giving.'

I don't respond but instead contemplate the idea of judgement casting the shadow, creating the imbalance. As we 'sin' or 'miss the mark', the shame that we are taught can feel torturous.

For a moment my mind is cast back to Europe in the thirties and the belief that evil was invading our shores in every sense of the word. I recall the images of Nazi Germany and the clarity of the perceived evil, in the form of symbols, uniforms and salutes, and how different everything is now, how subtle and sophisticated this shadowy force has become. However, the belief that this is some outside energy that is pervading our society has not changed. We are still in denial.

I search for the right words, hoping not to fall into the trap of more judgement. 'I would love to believe that the parts of you that are the beast is closer to G-d than the human, for the beast is without ego, without judgement and exists purely in the vibration of love.' I stop there, that's enough. I can already hear the bang of the gavel.

What was left in my mind was the knowing that my shadow was my failure to acknowledge my physical body in every sense of the word.

*   *   *

Towards the end of 2015, my parents were just moving out of their flat in the heart of Bristol which had been their home for over thirty years. It was on the top floor of a huge five-storey warehouse Dad had bought for his business in the seventies and it had become his mission to move out of there for the past fifteen years. As the deal was done and they moved into their new wonderful, garden flat, there were still a couple of things to collect from the old flat if we wanted.

Mark and I went up in the lift for the last time and took a huge garden ceramic pot that we wanted for our courtyard. As we pushed Dad's homemade wooden trolley onto the street and prepared to lift it into the boot of our car, I had a momentary lapse of reason. I have always had a strong back, working with bands and heavy equipment over the years has made me strong for my size. However, I'd forgotten that two years living in Frome had given me back problems. I lifted and twisted and crunch; that was it. I felt something go in my pelvis around my lower back.

'I'll be fine,' I said in my usual stuff and nonsense kind of way.

'You sure?' Mark wasn't sure and he was right not to be.

We eventually got back home after a pointless visit to our hospital. I got to my bed and promptly vomited. Not ever having broken any bones or had children, I'd never experienced pain like it. I was OK lying on my back but anything other than that wasn't so much as painful but just wrong at a core level. Simply attempting to sit up sent me into a kind of shock. My back went into spasms and my breath became fast and panicky. We immediately called Peter, the same therapist who put me to rights the last time and over the next ten days he gently put me back together again.

This time spent on my back allowed me to just be with myself, with my body. I was at last prepared to recognise that I had been holding onto tension in my arse since I was twenty-five, with my grandma's death and my asthma diagnosis. The fact that it can be so deep-seated that you cannot feel it unless something triggers it is an amazing metaphor for the mental pain we keep hidden from our awareness.

The last three years had intensified the stress I was putting on myself and as my mind was 'fine' with it all, my body just kept taking the load, until something had to give. After two warnings which I hadn't heeded, I could now see that if I wasn't going to do something about the disconnection between the Holy Trinity of my mind, body and spirit, something was going to be done for me.

Now the stress had been cracked open, releasing the energy that was stuck, frozen in me. The problem was that it couldn't get out, it was still trapped in my body. I envisaged it like an alien living inside me, like one of those terrible horror movies where you can see it moving just under the skin of some poor unfortunate soul.

Every day I'd wake up with it nestled in a different part of my body. One morning my jaw would be locked tight, another it would be in the back of my head, sometimes my arse or my chest, and so it went on. Eventually it took up a more permanent residence in my hip, though still enjoying the odd visits to other regions of my body when it chose. If it wasn't painful and tiring it would have been funny. Of course I laughed plenty and gradually it improved but there wasn't going to be any quick fix.

∗   ∗   ∗

During these quiet few days on my back I had time to take stock of things, to make peace with myself. I contemplated the years of not listening to my body, this amazing temple we are gifted to carry with us through life. Mine had borne so much and yet given me so little trouble.

A memory that pervaded my half-sleep, half-waking hours was of a talk I attended in St Stephen's around 2008. Two American authors, Rev Rita Nakashima Brock, PhD and Rev Dr Rebecca Parker, whose CVs were longer than my arm, had come to England to talk about their book called *Saving Paradise*. It was their mission to bring Christ down off the cross as a dominant image in our churches today. Of course, this resonated with me strongly.

Their research covered two areas. The first was the idea that before the Holy Wars in Palestine all the images of Christ in early churches were of Jesus as the teacher, the healer, the lamb. It was only after the Islamic invasions (from the seventh century) and the Christian crusades (from the twelfth century), when killing in the name of G-d was deemed acceptable, that we started to see this horrific image of pain and suffering in our churches.

Both women were also devoted to the study of psychology and how it overlaps with theology and their social activism. Through their work with women suffering abuse, both physical and sexual, they reached the painful conclusion that many women were returning to their abusive partners because they believed that pain and suffering was the way to redemption. In other words the image of Christ on the cross was teaching them that this would bring them closer to G-d. The messaging was clearly subliminal and the women only realised this concept after a great deal of therapy and psychological analysis.

It felt huge at the time but it was only through my explorations here did I remember that I had encountered subliminal messaging before with the cassettes on Satanism I listened to in Singapore. Now I felt impelled to join these women on their peaceful crusade.

What it also brought to mind was the need to fully address the issue of the Church taking a Middle Eastern man as their figurehead and changing the colour of his skin to wield their power in the racial battle we are engaged in. It's not that I hadn't thought about it before but I hadn't considered that any change was even possible until now.

I knew I had to be careful as my reactive mind wanted to judge the Church and label it as the beast, blocking out the view of its beauty. I contemplated my story of putting my own cross down alongside these two women dedicated to their mission. The guilt carried by Jews and instilled in Christians with the burden of Original Sin is something I've been trying to rid myself of all my life. Christian ministries, set up on the foundations of this belief, that keep making the choice of fear over love, have compelled me to question this ideology.

How should I move forward, work through the necessary healing while holding the awareness in my body? This would require a careful balancing act between a clear mind, a patient spirit and a self-aware body with strength at my core.

* * *

Soon after I was up and about, a talk was offered by a man, called Dominic Barter, who had set up a Restorative Justice project in Rio de Janeiro. This revolutionary process, working with people who commit criminal offences and those they harm, was now taking off in the UK and the police in some counties were keen to recruit volunteers.

He based his work on the idea that people are generally, in our society, not heard. If this becomes untenable then we lash out, create harm and too often stray from the path of righteousness.

If still nobody listens, then we are likely to continue to act in a way that will usually result in a prison sentence. In most cases, I don't believe that this is the answer.

People who are abused, and children in particular who are too young to understand what has happened to them, often feel that they are to blame or that it happened because they are a bad person. Sometimes, they deal with the pain they are holding onto inside by acting it out on others, especially if the abuse is recurrent and so 'normalised'. If this leads to a prison sentence, it just confirms their feelings of being a bad person.

Sadly, our conventional institutions don't have enough of the necessary procedures in place – nor a willingness to look deeper into healing the causes of criminal behaviour – to help many individuals work through their issues. When violent conflict occurs, it only finds the easiest solutions which are rarely the best. It simply points the finger, sees people who commit a 'sin' as a threat to the community and puts them behind a wall, in prison.

Once again, we think we are removing the problem. Unfortunately, when the sentence has been served and the so-called 'criminal' is released, they are often harder and angrier than ever when they re-enter society. Another wall and the Minotaur just keeps growing.

I believe these words from Kahlil Gibran's *The Prophet* offer another way of perceiving this:

> *'Speak to us of Crime and Punishment: Oftentimes have I heard you speak of one who commits a wrong as though he were not one of you, but a stranger unto you and an intruder upon your world.*
>
> *But I say as even as the holy and the righteous cannot*

rise beyond the highest which is in each one of you,
So the wicked and the weak cannot fall lower than the
lowest which is in you also.
And as a single leaf turns not yellow but with the silent
knowledge of the whole tree,
So the wrong-doer cannot do wrong without the
hidden will of you all.
Like a procession you walk together towards your god-
self.' [6]

Instead of recognising this idea of the unified soul, of humanity as a whole, we have travelled in the opposite direction into individualisation and separation. We have developed such extreme points of view, and an intolerance so strong, that any group that doesn't sit inside the image of what or how we see ourselves, must be removed. We have forgotten that this begins with our internal conflict, and this has extended beyond all boundaries engaging us in another world war without actually defining it as such; we are at war with ourselves.

In the midst of my struggle with this truth, Dominic Barter's talk showed me that something was changing within our penal system. I signed up to know more and trained to become a Restorative Justice facilitator. What I discovered was more than I possibly had bargained for.

Dominic created safe spaces with support for all parties where everyone listened to each other's stories and their pain. He found that empathy wins every time (except in cases of extreme psychopathic behaviour) and the hurt can be understood, acknowledged and often laid to rest.

What I found most exciting was that in some cases the person inflicting pain on others would, for the first time, engage with the effect they were having on people's life. While most people might find it difficult to believe that they wouldn't be aware of this, it is important to recognise that some people are so caught up in their world it takes extreme emotional experiences, like meeting the person they have harmed face to face, to realise the full impact of their actions. There are stories of people completely reforming their lives and one man, Peter Woolf, not only stopped committing crimes, he became a major campaigner for Restorative Justice. (Please see Further References.)

I now know that I am not alone in believing that this is how our prison population will be reduced; not with harder sentences.

*   *   *

It was a tough year. Everyone remembers 2016 for the loss of so many artists and generally well-loved people. David Bowie was a huge blow, one of my greatest inspirations, and there were many others that followed. But the year continued, as it had started on a more personal level.

Mark's mother had been ill for years with a heartbreaking degenerative disease. When his father died, over two years previously, we were all amazed that he had gone first.

As May approached, it was clear it was her time. One Sunday morning, Mark's stepdad gathered her two sons to her bedside. I stood with them, quietly witnessing their pain while we watched her gently slip away. When she drew her last breath, we only realised it was, when she failed to take another. A profound, poignant silence followed and I felt honoured to have been present.

As if it wasn't hard enough for the family, that month her younger brother was diagnosed with a brain tumour. The funeral held many mixed emotions for all and by the autumn he too had gone.

The autumn also brought another big loss with the death of a musician I had recently started playing with in Frome. He was one of the pillars of the community, who helped youngsters with their musical ambitions as well as dedicating years of his work to restorative justice. He was a man ahead of his time and a joy to play music with.

To be honest the whole six months were a bit of a blur, but the most significant moment happened in August. Mark and I had just returned from my friend's beautiful handfasting in North Wales. We arrived home tired but happy, glad to have been a part of a momentous occasion in my friend's life. I was just climbing into bed thinking I'd have a short nap before my gig that night, when the phone went and it was Mum telling me that Dad had just died.

It was unbelievable. He was perfectly well, in full health just the day before. But, it was obviously his time. He and Mum had moved into the small flat, he had finished putting up all the shelves and cupboards, got everything in order and now he had fulfilled his mission he could go.

A few years before he had told Mark, 'When I go it'll be like that!' He snapped his fingers. Mark had felt the poignancy of the memory as he had known exactly what he meant at the time. But so soon, it seemed unreal, especially as he had no ailments and never had any. He simply ate something that disagreed with his stomach and it was too much for him. He gently slipped away in a matter of hours, just how he wanted it.

The speed and yet the simplicity of it meant my tears came in unexpected moments but they were usually brief and fairly contained. We had a few days' grace to get the funeral preparations together but it never seems like long enough. Many

Jewish funerals happen the next day, we had seven. I couldn't help feeling that, having reached ninety-three, if I hadn't done some preparation for his departure, with all my work with death over the past ten or so years, then what did I think I was doing? I knew I had said all I wanted to say, I'd told him I loved him and dealt with the family cultural conflicts I had created and resolved through my play. All was well. It was harsh and incredibly painful but I couldn't have wished for a more perfect passing for him.

The rabbi who took the service was a young man and spoke beautifully. His ideas seemed to sit alongside mine far more than I would have expected. Jewish funerals are usually very dismal affairs. Many Christian funerals I'd attended were full of singing and heartfelt eulogies; there was none of that here, just a few words my sisters and I prepared. We dearly hoped we did him justice; Dad was such a good speech-maker.

That night, completely exhausted after making all those cups of tea and sandwiches with my sisters, I thought I'd try something. Still carrying some pain in my hip after my back incident eight months before, I called out to my dad,

'Now you're there and I'm here perhaps you have a little more idea of what I've been trying to talk to you about for the past few years?' We had enjoyed a few healing swaps almost a decade earlier, but I had left Dad to it after that. Now I felt I could connect with him on this level and maybe have the chance of working with my grandparents. 'Would it be OK if I attempted to do another healing with you?' I asked.

As I lay on my bed, I placed Dad in front of me, imagining all my ancestors lined up behind him. I tried to avoid my image of Jacob's ladder skidding around on a unicycle, as I didn't think this would be appropriate. I breathed into the energy and asked if anything could be done for the low level but continual pain in my hip I'd been carrying throughout the year.

I had no idea what happened but when I woke the next morning the pain had gone. I offered up a huge thank you. This was the first of a few opportunities I had to release some of the pain and tension from my body.

The year continued and so did the losses, it felt like we were just getting over one while we were holding our breath for the next. We didn't really relax till December and I use the term 'relax' very loosely. My body was anything but that at this point.

How do you come to terms with the loss of your father, someone who has been a guiding hand through fifty years of your life? His quiet but sure nature held the family together and his presence was inevitably going to be vastly missed. However, what held me through the coming months was the fact that my father always told me how he spoke to his parents daily, both having died fairly young.

I naturally wanted to continue his tradition and as time progressed I would invite him in to any situation I thought he might enjoy experiencing. I felt him chuckling and his words, 'Well, who would have thought,' echo in my head, as I sat him next to me during a meditation session or a Restorative Justice meeting.

I was hoping for a healing to end all healings, the moment when I would be able to create the final release and remove the alien from my body. However, it took me a while to realise the universe had other plans for me. I had acknowledged that lifting the garden pot was not a mistake, but a gift. As I was put back together by my back therapist, he realigned me in a way I had never been aligned before and set me on a new road, a whole new journey.

People, already way ahead of me on this adventure, were coming into my life. This started to feel like a great surge of energy erupting through the foundations of our society; the earthquake, that I saw in my meditation nearly twenty years ago, appearing in the cracks of our bodies. Physical and emotional strength was certainly going to be required.

*   *   *

2017 came as a relief. Ringing in the new year, I put out a prayer for a more peaceful, less stressful time ahead.

A noise from the shadows I recognise.

'OK, I hear you. I know that publishing my book and CD, commissioning a music video and putting my band back together amounts to a major task. I organised gigs, book launches and magazine reviews and most of the marketing.'

'Not stressful at all.'

'I didn't think you did sarcasm,' I pointed out.

'Just mirroring you,' it spoke in all innocence.

Although the project was really well received I felt my audiences did not match the huge amount of energy I had put in and I was trying not to feel disappointed by it all; my drawbridge was still up. I needed to remind myself that what mattered more was that everyone (with only one exception) who read the book or heard the CD was very moved and some people found it deeply transformational.

Running alongside this was also my new work as a Restorative Justice facilitator. Life was full yet again.

The summer brought some powerful healings. One showed me that the only thing that stood between myself and my ability to connect with my higher self, which has been my holy grail since I discovered it was possible twenty years ago, was me. My desperation and obsession was the block and the irony was laughable. I can only learn this the hard way, it seems.

'I could have told you that.' There is a gentleness in my Minotaur's voice and my heart relaxes when it enters the space now.

'I know, and in a way you did,' I smile at the thought, 'when I turn to you, there you are with the answers. When I turn away, there you are, still holding them for when I'm ready to turn back.'

*　*　*

The anniversary of my father's death passed, celebrated by the setting of the stone, without a great deal of fuss. In the months that followed I found myself on the mailing list of my rabbi. I don't remember signing up but there it was in my inbox every few weeks inviting me to some Jewish ceremony or festival. Slowly it sunk into my awareness and one day I found myself responding.

'Do you meet with your flock, even if they have left?' I asked. I was just seeking some fatherly advice. This rabbi, I discovered, was from a strain of Judaism I'd not heard of before, called Chabad, the name coming from the Kabbalistic tree of life. He was very interested in drawing back in those who had strayed.

We met in a cafe I knew well in Bristol and he gave me an hour of his precious time. The cafe was busy but we found a table in the corner. Although he wore some distinguishing garments, as a rabbi, nobody took particular heed of him. I was glad, I didn't want to be distracted as he started imparting a good deal of information to me. I spoke about my atheist upbringing and my spiritual journey that followed much later but how I felt the need to learn more about my roots to integrate them into my life.

Whatever I mentioned, just like Tim Higgins from St Stephen's Church, he referred it back to his teachings. I was most surprised when he even agreed with my belief in reincarnation. I had never heard of Jews being open to that concept before. He suggested that I found a few things that resonated with my own beliefs that married with some Jewish traditions, so I began lighting candles on Friday nights, I put money in a box for charity regularly to grow my abundance and recognised the prayers of gratitude that mirrored mine in my own daily meditation practice.

Rabbi Mendy spoke of Abraham, Isaac and Jacob. He explained how each man's life related to a Kabbalistic way of being that reflected the time. Abraham, being Chessed, meaning kindness, Isaac, being Gevurah, meaning strength and Jacob, Tiferet, meaning beauty. He mentioned that we were now returning to a time of kindness. This made my heart sing, once more.

I left the cafe feeling full, full of my sense of history and my connection to it but also sadness that so much has been lost. When so much pain and persecution is experienced, it often feels simpler to shake off the religious shackles that this brings into our lives. Although it may offer a feeling of safety, over the years it left me feeling bereft. I needed to bring in these new rituals and wrap myself up in the healing that embodying the new with the old offered. I am very grateful to my rabbi for this.

It has taken me many years but now I have a whole different sense of what these ancient ceremonies truly mean. After having lived in a place that felt empty for so long it helped me expand my exploration into what that empty space can really mean; one that is full of the fecundity of life, of G-d.

I was building a new relationship with these rituals, both Jewish and spiritual. Though I still felt uncomfortable with the

Jewish religion, running away from it all came at a cost. What I was dealing with now was healing the damage this journey of separation may have incurred on the way as I cut my ties with my ancestors and the years in the desert that followed.

I started to question how, from my Semitic Jewish ancestry, I had, in the present day apparently become 'white'. This skin-deep new suit many Jews had donned was pushing us further away from our roots, further into disconnect. Mirroring the world, as I have said, we are being asked to choose in the moment what we are going to do with the path we have taken. Falling into the trap of moving further away from G-d as so many Jews left the religion after the pain the Holocaust brought us, we set up the new homeland built on the pain we endured and so continued the cycle of oppression on others. If the Jews were chosen to find our way back to G-d for the rest of humanity to watch and learn we are certainly choosing the hardest way there.

Still far from home, I longed for the love to pour through my veins, to massage the muscles and oil the joints of the ancestral tree that feeds me. Gradually, as my body began to respond to the healing and breathe again, I found myself on the shores of my next journey; learning how to release the cause of asthma and other issues that are born out of our cultural story using Somatics.[7]

* * *

Towards the end of 2017 I finally found my way to the TreeSisters website, an organisation that 'inspires restoration by rapidly accelerating tropical reforestation through feminine leadership'. This had been calling me for some time but was something I had kept resisting. Somehow trees didn't feel that important to me.

What's the expression?

'You couldn't see the wood for the trees?' My Minotaur helpfully interjected.

'OK, so this was huge and the whole wisdom of Mother Nature contained in a single, beautiful metaphorical image began to unfold like worlds within worlds.'

I learned how the tree perfectly represented every living being in our universe. The torus[8], is a self-sustaining, self-perpetuating energy force. It flows up from its base, the roots, through the central core of its being and then, as it reaches the top, or the crown, falls like a fountain back down to the bottom again feeding back into the root system once more. We are like this, our Earth, galaxy and our entire universe, even our individual cells mirror this model, like Russian dolls.

'And do you see how this works for our journey through the ages?' My teacher is guiding me yet again. 'You see how the flow can be seen as a journey through time, your favourite subject?'

I laugh, 'go on, throw it at me.'

'So we begin our journey in the Garden of Eden, all those thousands of years ago, living in harmony with everything in the core of our being in the roots and the trunk of the tree. Then we travel away, without blame, from our source, creating a state of separation, of duality. Here the branches separate, often into three and the disconnection continues taking us even further away from home as we keep splitting apart, from the existing three branches into the separate branches and twigs. This reflects our journey into the three religions and then all the different denominations and ways of separation we create in our society.'

I can't help myself from jumping in, 'and now we have moved into the world of the individual, the ego-led lifestyle we are now hanging off the edge of each twig as individual leaves.' I stop short. 'Oh, but now there's only one way to go.'

'As autumn comes to its natural end, it is the way of all things.'

'But,' I am desperate to find another route, 'but surely we can do the work, there must be an alternative? I believe we can climb back down from the top of the tree and do the reconciliation work at each point of separation and make our way back to our hearts.'

'Ever the optimist.' My Minotaur sighs, 'you'll need to heal the rifts between the atheists and their rejection of religion and between all the religions. If you surrender to the fall you'll all arrive at the same place. It'll require far less effort, like the film *Sliding Doors*, different paths, same outcome.'

'I know but all that loss and pain, I really struggle with that.' I feel myself fidget with discomfort at the whole idea.

'So how else are you going to do this?'

'Like you say,' I am buoyed by its insistence, 'I am the eternal optimist. Bucket loads of hard work, I can handle emotional pain, if it is handled and transmuted with care that is.' I pause. 'We just have to remember, there's a field, beyond right and wrong. I'll meet you there.'

PART 2

I decide to take a bit of time out. I can see the end in sight, but my desire to get home safely is weighing heavily on my shoulders. I had put down the cross, but had I picked up some other trials on my way without noticing, yet again?

I let myself drop into my surroundings and realise that the greenery in this petal is growing, rewilding all by itself, but at a distance. I try to feel into, breathe in its lusciousness. How could

I remove this feeling of separation and then once connected how could I keep hold of it?

So many times I have experienced moments of complete release, into the arms, the abundance of universal love, only to come away from that moment to pick up the stresses of being disconnected all over again. It's like an old heavy blanket I truly no longer want or need but habitually carry around with me, or a spring that's set to a high tension within the core of my being. When met by a high vibration of love, it can totally uncoil, but it soon springs back once the wave has passed, like an internal preset button.

We can experience revelation, by forgiving or being forgiven, our hearts may be opened for a short while, but to stay on the path, that takes real strength. Having discovered that strength is found in softness, in feeling everything; being vulnerable maybe a powerful place but it's not an easy state to maintain. I needed help.

The images and revelations that trees, as they mirror life, offered me kept deepening, creating layer upon layer of new wisdom. My Minotaur had taught me about our cultural journey into separation and the next step took just a small mental leap to realise that this was our individual journey too.

The tree reflects our own journey from our roots and heart up into our head. The separation occurs and as our minds become the master rather than the slave, we lose the connection to, and the wisdom of, our hearts. As we reach further for the sky into the extremity of our egos, our individuality makes us feel like a king, but really we are the fool, like a lost child longing to return home.

While it's not for me to bring the Leo lion's egotistical pride to a fall, my fear is that if we fail to make that choice by ourselves, it will forced upon us. The only thing I can do right now is to make the necessary preparations and start the journey back home myself with every gentle step of reconciliation that falls in my path.

*   *   *

After launching my first book, I was invited to join a writers' boot camp. This was a three month-long weekly gathering where twenty or so writers could get feedback on their work. It was very enriching and took place in some beautiful locations around Frome. The first session was to start within the week of the Frome Festival.

One night, at one of the local festival hangouts, I bumped into one of my Jewish friends, Elaine, who reminded me that there was a group of Jewish ladies who met for lunch in Bath a few times a year. The next meeting coincided with the first day of the boot camp and the timings overlapped a little. Elaine offered to pick me up straight from the venue to save time. It was a deal.

I arrived at the boot camp, excited and a little apprehensive but the gardens were beautiful and I knew plenty of the other authors there. I settled in and presented this book, the second in my trilogy, which was still in its early stages. I had just spent the last twelve months rewriting, publishing and marketing my first book. This one, which I had started a couple of years before, had been put on hold. I was ready to step deeper into the process of the labyrinth.

It was an enjoyable morning, the first of many, and I soon got over my nervousness of bearing my thoughts and ideas as others bore theirs.

Leaving promptly, Elaine and a friend were waiting for me

at the end of the drive and we hurried to Bath. The meeting was at a popular cafe and the room, with its wooden chairs and hard furnishings, was fairly noisy. Conversations were limited to just your neighbours. I was seated next to an elderly lady, called Friedel, who was lively and interesting, but it wasn't until people started peeling away that I struck up a more in-depth conversation with her. She began to tell me her life story.

'I was five when the need to leave Germany became an imperative and I was put on the list for the Kinder transport.' My eyes widened as realised she was about to embark on quite a tale. I quickly stepped up my level of listening. I learned that the Kinder transport wasn't able to simply pull the children out of countries in which they were in danger, they could only leave if they had families to go to.

There was a family in Bristol looking for a child and Friedel was second on the list to a Polish girl. Her big sister was too old as the family wanted a child that would be younger than their own. It just happened at that time that Hitler declared that all foreign children living in Germany should go home to their countries of origin. This put Friedel at the top and she arrived safely in England where she spent the rest of her life.

When the war ended, there began the whole business of connecting families back together again. Friedel discovered that only her aged grandmother had survived where all the other members of her family had perished.

I listened intently, knowing that her accent together with the bad acoustics made it difficult to gather all the details. As her story unfolded, my heart felt like it might burst as this gentle woman talked to me in such a matter of fact manner. I fought to hold back the tears. How could I cry when the storyteller was so calm and collected?

She continued speaking about her visit to her grandma in a home in Holland. Friedel explained how, after returning home to the UK, she heard her grandmother, seeing that her granddaughter was alive and well, had let go of her need to continue her life and died a week later. It took all my self-control to hold myself together as she spoke.

The conversation turned to me and we talked a little about music and then Friedel said that she couldn't sing. I told her that I wasn't surprised, having gone through such a journey but explained that this is what I loved to do; help people find their voice. She laughed, thinking it was unlikely but agreed to give it a go. I left promising to be in touch. In the months that followed we embarked on a delicate and courageous process. Friedel, trusting me to help her take her first step, succeeded with surprising ease and little or no trauma attached to it.

When I got home, following our first luncheon meeting, I went straight upstairs to my meditation room, sat for minute in silence and reverence for this woman of such strength and grace, before sobbing my heart out.

I then realised I hadn't really thought the whole layout of the day properly. It was now about five o'clock. Frome Festival is always a busy week and I had booked tickets to go to an event hosted by the Frome Friends of Palestine.

I had moved on from being active in the group, needing to put my energy into writing. The Frome Writer's Collective had taken me on as trustee; another new role out of my comfort zone. However, I always made an effort to attend the FFoP's fundraising events and especially their contribution in the festival. After giving me a support slot to Seize the Day, I was very pleased when they booked one of my own bands the following year.

This year I had been too busy to investigate what Mark and I had bought tickets for, other than knowing it was a play called *Love, Bombs and Apples*. As I took my seat, I remembered the Jewish stand-up comic they put on last time. I had no idea what to expect.

It was a one-man show, a young Muslim actor, playing four short acts. The first three were stories of young Muslim men. Each piece was witty, intelligent and very pertinent. However, in the final piece he played a young American Jewish man, struggling to keep the peace between his liberal Jewish girlfriend who is horrified by the actions of the Israeli government and his father, a traditional American Jew who has his patter down to a tee. If you criticise the Israeli government then you must be antisemitic; if you are a Jew who does this then you are a traitor.

I felt the words cut through me like a knife. This issue had been sitting with me for a few years now and here it was being beautifully played out in front of me with humour and delicacy. I wanted to grab him and kiss him. More, I wanted to get him on every stage and relevant Internet site possible.

I returned home feeling relieved but completely exhausted. I had only just reopened my book after a brief time away and now there was no closing it again. I felt this day was significant, giving my journey a kick start and myself the strength to stay the course to bring it to fruition.

*   *   *

In 2018 I read the *Gospel of Mary*. There I found great treasures; it being, in itself, a lost treasure. This gospel, that has only just recently been discovered and translated, reaffirms my feeling that now we are entering a time of great significance with the chance of receiving the true teachings of Christ. I believe that 2,000 years ago we were given a choice. Jesus, who represented the messiah in all of us, was showing us a way. However, we were not ready and we buried the truth for when the time would be right.

Once again the words of my friend, Seb, that we will be asked to choose between the shadow or the light, reminded me that this has been our story at every juncture in history. Making good decisions takes great strength and courage. When we continue to make decisions that do not serve us, that miss the mark, we have to learn to be patient, to understand the bigger story at play here. Jumping to anger or frustration doesn't help, it just adds to the negative vibration of the world. Holding faith and trusting that all will be well has kept me on track.

It speaks of how Mary Magdalene and Peter dealt with the death and resurrection of Jesus, how Mary received Jesus with grace and without fear. This was because she had grasped his teachings well enough to no longer be his pupil – which is the nature of a good teacher – but be in full understanding of her spiritual self as he was. This could be seen as a reason why he came to her first after his resurrection.

When she tells the other disciples of her encounter with the spirit of Christ, Peter becomes angry and scared. Peter has not gained enough wisdom to understand and respond positively to the presence of Jesus, the fact that he visited a woman first, nor the tasks he asked of his disciples. It is Peter's reactions that have been passed down to us through his teaching as he overpowered Mary and drew the other disciples into fear. This, I feel, is the Minotaur in the Christian faith.

Sadly, Mary's teaching of love, as the continuation of Christ's words, got buried (along with Thomas's, whose gospel also reveals the true depth of his teaching).

However, the gospel reminded me that people in leadership roles, political or religious, are just mirroring the culture as a whole. This is why we are now taught history in schools rather than her story and what grieves me more, her story has been twisted to be considered as heresy.

For the last 2,000 years we have been living with this inheritance, under the domination and fear of the masculine, having lost its divinity, which has, in turn, suppressed, and slowly removed from our culture, the divine feminine. This has been done in the most terrible, protracted way with the witch hunts; the burning and drowning of women. Witches were, of course, simply wise women with an understanding of herbs and medicines, the healing of our bodies in a way that is in tune with nature.

Of course it's important to avoid getting into the battle of the sexes, believing that all women were wise and good and all men were oppressors. This is the kind of extremist beliefs we find being hurled around today. All men and women can be all things. However, while it is the gender balance in all of us I am exploring, it is important to acknowledge that it was mainly the women who bore, and still bear, the burden of being physically oppressed (#notallmen).[9]

The fear and brutality of this massacre, the denial of ourselves and the judgment of others to save ourselves, has left deep scars in both women and men. We have created laws out of this brutality.

The *Gospel of Mary* says:

'Law, it would seem, is set up to work on the side of those who wish to enslave the soul. The soul's refusal to judge is also a refusal to be bound by their unjust and ignorant laws.' [10]

Only the ego judges, and when it looks through this lens, it creates a society, a G-d, a religion and a culture, that carries judgement at its core. But who is to say what is good and what is bad, which right and which wrong? When someone sins is it not possible that, 'he is doing the best he can, given the limits of his consciousness?' In the yin yang symbol each section has a dot of the opposite colour at the centre of it. Each holds the opposite way of being at its heart, for one is created out of the other and neither can be wholly separated from each other.

Once again we see the Minotaur in our world; which part is the beauty and which the beast?

All three religions were birthed out of pure love, but the beauty of the original teaching can easily be lost. Through the ages there are always those capable of seeing through the fog of corruption and translation, and embody the original truth, but there are many who cannot. What if no one judged, maybe we'd all be set free?

When we legislate against challenging behaviour in our culture; racism, sexism, oppression we believe we have solved these issues and often we can see the improvements it brings. However, this is usually in the good times.

I believe that simply telling people not to think in a certain way because it's bad will not change the way they feel. On the surface they may not show those feelings for fear of being penalised, and they may speak of believing that these laws are right. But, when cornered or scared the amygdala[11], deep within the temporal lobe of our brain, kicks in before our conscious brain knows there has been a reaction. No laws, no good training can stem that knee-jerk reaction of pain, whatever our creed or colour.

We have all been taught to mistrust, belittle and overpower the 'other' in our lives. This is born out of a simple need for self-preservation in this harsh world in which we find ourselves and our ego's need to rule the heart.

I believe, this inner war, which started when we left the Garden of Eden and the three Abrahamic religions split apart, can only end when we choose to return to the garden, to our hearts. We can only do this by reconciling this rift that is cut into the roots of our ancestral stories. We have to rewrite the inscriptions.

I returned to the Hero's Journey to help me envision a fast track version of the story of humanity from the European perspective. Our journey began in the Rift Valley. We travelled across the world, changing and adapting to our environment over hundreds of thousands of years, until arriving in the West with archetypal white skin and blue eyes. Along the way we became farmers and consumers, separated from ourselves and our connection to the physical and spiritual world.

When we took to the seas 500 years ago, we ventured out as Imperialist 'exploiters' and missionaries. The Holy Wars fought and won, we brought the Christian message as we journeyed back home to the shores of Africa and faced some of our original selves in their free and fully heart-centred way of being. Fear must have been the first emotion, quickly followed by a sense of superiority and a fierce need to 'civilise' or enslave the people they found.

Once again, as with the issues between the sexes, I am not wanting to point the finger in any direction. We can all be all things, but I am simply attempting to tease out the story that has brought us to this place of imbalance of racial power in our culture (#notallwhites).

The story of the Jews, I believe, is the same story compressed into 2,000 years. We changed from a people of Middle Eastern,

Semitic skin colour and assimilated into the white Western race (for those who travelled north rather than south). Some returned home facing their brothers and sisters. The fear and suppressed emotions held in their bodies and psyche as they arrived is playing its part in the conflict we have today.

The Jews, believing themselves to be the 'chosen' people are holding up the mirror, reflecting their journey for all humanity, for doesn't everybody believe themselves to be, and isn't everybody, chosen. What choices are we going to make when we arrive back home?

For those who believe we can only return to the homeland when we have peace in our hearts, some Jews have returned too soon, when they are not truly ready. Still holding onto their trauma and fear, are they killing their brother for revealing their feelings of disconnection, mirroring their newly adopted European story? What will it take for them to step back into love and embrace them with open arms? When we choose to arrive back into the oneness of our hearts, we will discover that not only all members of these three faiths are our brothers and sisters but also all the peoples of the world.

However painful it is to write this, this cliché we constantly turn our backs on, the fact is that while we remain unaware of our sense of separation from all things at a base level, it still needs to be stated, over and over again. We have been trained to see the 'other' as our enemy by the misinterpretation of religious text, and the manipulation of our penal and legal systems. This has kept the fire of hatred alight.

It is time for us to recognise this. For me, what takes strength is knowing that this journey back to love is about the long game. I have learned through the writing of these words that patience is a huge part of being strong. If we rise to anger and try and pull down the structures that rule our lives too soon, before the new infrastructure is in place, we will create chaos. Everything is happening in perfect order and the green shoots are already appearing. They will soon gather momentum but things that are rushed have no foundations. We need good foundations.

There are many ways to ride this tidal wave whether we take the inner journey or step into action. There is much to do to prepare the way, as long as we remember that everything happens in its own time and that faith keeps us strong and our strength can shore up our faith.

There is a little part of me that believes that once enough momentum has been gathered the new world we all yearn for will just appear as the old one will simply fall away and this hard work I am speaking of will be no longer necessary. We can all dream but isn't it our dreams that shape our reality?

The future might look bleak, or bright depending on your choices. In the meanwhile, the one thing I believe I have come here to do is to blow my bugle, summon people to join me in bringing down the walls of judgement and move towards the future with a positive and open heart.

* * *

TreeSisters also have a six stage journey. The first is called Reveal, where we step into the crown of our heads, open to the higher energies and ask for guidance. If we are willing to understand that we know nothing of the vast wisdom of the universe, start from that point of being an empty vessel, we can be open to the possibility of being filled with new divine understanding. This is a feminine act and has much to do with being able to say, 'I don't know'; a revelation and a relief for many people.

As we stepped into 2019 it felt like the world was embracing a new kind of energy. Extinction Rebellion had recently announced itself to the world, and this movement was gathering with it a global community wishing to deal with the potentially unsurmountable issue of our ecological crisis. It was practising the radical methods of love and peace. Ignoring history, for those who try this usually meet their demise, it came from a desire for evolution rather than revolution. Not knowing where this new way of rebelling would take us, filled me with optimism. I knew nothing would be the same again.

For the April protest in London, Mark and I decided to join for one day, just to dip our toes in. When we arrived on the first day, Waterloo Bridge, which had been designated for the South West contingent, had already been taken, along with five others. The sun was shining and there was music, dancing, acrobatics and good food. The mood was incredible.

In the weeks leading up to this protest, I had been rehearsing with a group of singers. Once on the bridge, we started warming up. After a few chants, we started singing a Seize the Day song. From nowhere, two women joined our circle and seemed to know all the words. But it wasn't till we finished that one of them took off their sunglasses and I exclaimed, 'Oh, hi Shannon!' Seize the Day were here.

It felt like one big festival. It was only as we were returning home at the end of the day that the tone of the rebellion started to change as the arrests began. But it was the beginning of something very exciting; a new intelligent form of resistance, a transformational energy that had a world wide web of connection in more than sixty countries.

Two weeks later I received a text from Shannon, 'would you like to join the band?' It felt like my career had reached its zenith. An exciting fusion of my musical endeavours and my new energy for politics and activism, this band brought it all together. I also felt that Frome had brought me full circle, a six-year journey, from my support gig in the Frome Festival where the band first came aware of my existence, to this wonderful way our lives were brought back together again.

A glorious summer of festival gigs followed. Performing with this band was inspiring, some songs often drew me to tears. That autumn, Extinction Rebellion was back on the streets. The bridge and equipment allotted to the South West had been blocked and confiscated respectively, so we found ourselves right in the heart of the rebellion. Instead of playing on a stage, we moved, with a portable sound system, to wherever there was a gathering. We sang to everyone from protesters to bystanders to those who had locked on and the police. It was exhilarating, and felt far more effective than any performance on a stage, this was massively empowering.

After three gruelling years of planning Brexit, yet another great splitting apart, Extinction Rebellion came as a great relief. However, it was quickly moved aside in 2020 by Covid-19. I wondered about the huge repercussions of this pandemic and how they will be felt for many years to come. Though we are often slow to understand the lessons, with so many people keen to get 'back to normal', I was constantly looking for the bigger picture. If we, as a society, recognised that the issues around isolation, and the economic, social, mental and emotional suffering it creates, was already in our culture like a virus, could we see that Covid-19 is purely highlighting this?

This moment also brought Black Lives Matter into our awareness, one climbing on the back of the other; a perfect opportunity for some potential healing in the great pause the pandemic offered. It seemed to me that this was a call out; a cry that demanded an answer. It had been around for some years before, but it took the death of yet another African American for the white communities everywhere to begin to understand the existing effects of white privilege and power. I learned to appreciate that everyone can be prejudiced but people can only be racist if they hold power; only those who are in a position of privilege can oppress others in social and political environments.

It felt like a light was being shone on this huge problem and, given twenty-twenty vision, we were being offered a deeper understanding of the oppression and the generations of collective trauma that have been built into our modern world like bricks and mortar.

Throughout the lockdown, I kept returning to the expression that through limitation comes expansion and sat with it a while. That summer, limited to connecting through online platforms, I joined a Conflict Transformation Summit where we were encouraged to bring our offerings. My play had been sitting in a drawer for five years so I decided to pull together an impromptu reading. The participants, who were scattered all over the world, saw a potential in the process it took the audience through, and encouraged me to turn it into a film. During its production, as the gifts flooded in, I wondered if this might be the seed for my next journey.

One gift, was the work of Etty Hillesum, whose diaries came into my awareness like the peeling back of the chairs in Chartres Cathedral. I read of her determination to find meaning rather than engage in collective hatred, her light and humanity that acted as a balm to all those who knew her. She remained deeply centred in her heart through all the dark days in Westerbork, a transit camp in which the Nazis concentrated the Dutch Jews, and even as she was being transported to Auschwitz. These revelations felt like another dissenting voice that had been silenced. We have all heard of Anne Frank, how deep do we have to dig to discover Etty's radical love?

Another gift not only helped me move forward but also felt like a consolidation of my explorations. It was David Baddiel's book *Jews Don't Count*, where he, in a timely way, highlighted the idea that Jews are rarely considered when it comes to racial discrimination compared to other ethnic minorities. He also examines the paradox where Jews are believed to be 'somehow both sub-human and humanity's secret masters', both inferior and superior, scorned and celebrated, though the favourable aspects are rarely offered with a positive inflection.

This, I believe, is how a society suffering internal conflict, views itself; the ego suppressing the heart. I sense that this is the way we feel about ourselves; we are all subliminally taught to believe that we are superior to 'others' and yet our propensity for self-hatred can be overwhelming. This felt huge.

It became increasingly clear to me that the story of the Jewish people, and particularly those who have returned to the homeland, and the complexity of being both the victim and the oppressor as a mirror for all, would be an excellent place to put my energy.

Our ability to 'other' every aspect of our world, to judge and hate, creating divisions from these frozen states in our body, devoid of empathy is juxtaposed against the kindness and love that we can all show and the paradox held in this tension. We are all of these things, the best and the worst, the love and the fear. We are all victims of collective trauma and very few are even aware of the subliminal messaging that prevents us from letting go, that has been hard-wired into our subconscious for too long; a new level of enquiry is required.

* * *

My Minotaur was not far away, still out of view, but an energy flowed between us, open, no longer an unknown. The way ahead was not going to be easy, but with a renewed sense of my destiny, I felt I had an ally rather than an enemy alongside me.

Strength and resilience were the necessary ingredients for this new recipe I was cooking up, and a big dose of kindness towards myself as well as others.

'Why do we still find that so hard?' I mused.

'Because as a culture you're so reluctant to do the inner work,' my Minotaur replies. 'Let's face it, it isn't pretty and for a people addicted to feeling good it's never going to sound like a ball of fun. Unfortunately there is no way around, you have to work through me, through your fears. Until you really get the magical interconnectivity of the idea of oneness, living a life with kindness at its heart is far too simple for your complicated mindset.'

'Ouch!' I feel the accuracy of its words.

Personally, it feels like our society is tying itself up in knots. Our disconnect with the land has led us to destroy the very thing that can teach and heal us if we'd only stop and listen. Our scientific world, bereft of any sense of empathy and love, is now being asked to solve problems it has itself created due to this lack. The Internet, instead of reminding us that we are all cosmically attuned to the beautiful web of life, is spinning truths and untruths like indiscernible threads. This echo chamber of chaos, confusion and torment, is simply mirroring ourselves back to us.

I recall my thoughts at the outset of this journey; that we can know our forward memory just as we are aware of our past. This is a gift and one we have dire need of now. How would I imagine our future?

I see a society turning the inward-looking microscope around and seeing with telescopic eyes once more, becoming the witness. A society that understands that it cannot survive where power and privilege is held by the few and so chooses to make 'divide and rule' a thing of the past.

I imagine a world where systems shift from a pyramidal structure to a flowing, living torus, where the Church, governments and corporations are no longer corrupt and abusive because the populace have discovered the concept of 'power with' rather than 'power over'; the fountain of our cultural wealth will begin to flourish once again. As we begin to understand oppression, its subtleties and clandestine deception, and how it reflects the inner journey we are all taking, we will stop blaming others and choose to heal together.

When we, like many aboriginal peoples, have ten 'dos' rather than ten 'don'ts', and judgement is no longer about accusation, and all about discernment, then we, I feel, will start to breathe again.

My dream is that we put down the chainsaw and remember how to connect with the power of the acorn. We stop trawling the oceans for its fruit, using it as a depository for our toxic waste, and bathe in its beauty. We surrender into the limitless bowl that Mother Nature weaves and fills for our pleasure.

Here we rediscover balance, the masculine and feminine find an equilibrium and we remember our wholeness, that just being ourselves is enough. This is, I believe, the Christ consciousness latent within us all. When we are ready to feel it, this will be the second coming.

The return to the homeland will be for all, not just the Jews, where home is a place of equality, diversity, respect and of course, love. This second coming, offered to all humanity, will not be some person coming to Earth to save us all, but our individual and collective opportunity to save ourselves.

I had heard of a workshop where this was treated as an exercise, where you journeyed into the future and created the world you would like to inhabit. The idea was that as you returned to the reality of the present you would feel bereft at the tremendous loss of this potential. Anyone who participates in this exercise will feel the sense of yearning we all have deep in our hearts, a feeling so powerful but equally so repressed. Once experienced it is rarely forgotten and would hopefully inspire us to constantly strive to bring this imagined way into our lives. Our refusal to acknowledge these feelings of deep longing keeps us disconnected from our empathy and ability to make the necessary changes in our hearts and lives.

The sixth and last stage of the TreeSisters' journey, after the feminine and masculine energies within us have been balanced, is called Belong. This returning to a state of reconnection brings me back to the image and metaphor of the tree. I see the rings representing our capacity for love and kindness, that some can only love those in their inner ring, those closest to them; their kin. As we expand our hearts we can bring more and more people into our circle of love, our kind, our nation, our creed or all of humanity. My hope is that as we heal we can grow in every sense of the word until we are all held in the outermost ring where we all belong.

I am aware that is about the long game and will require huge amounts of resilience for those developing their capacity to feel more. In the meantime, I worry that those who are not ready to connect to the emotional wisdom in their bodies, keep rushing into answers using their head without engaging the heart. When we think we have no time, our inability to stay centred keeps us distracted and off course. Our addiction to short-term solutions, knowledge, rather than wisdom, sensing our separation, rather than the collective, keeps breaking us apart. I believe, this is all part of the balancing act we are journeying towards.

The Elders of our world, our indigenous people, who have retained the universal wisdom gained over millennia, have prophecies that have foretold this whole journey. Despite being massacred, persecuted, forced off their land and their customs forcibly denied them, like parents waiting for their children to mature, they have been waiting for us to be ready to begin processing the healing journey with them.

The awareness that the wisdom we need is already here gives me great hope. I am always excited to discover that there are people who know how to listen to the land and receive its healing. There are also people who are developing science, a new kind that sees through the wide lens, to heal our soil, produce clean energy and live in harmony with our world. *For those who have the eyes to see and ears to hear* it is time to reawaken the understanding of the feminine and let her stand up and shine with all her heart.

We need to stop, slow down and breathe.

*   *   *

Through my musings there has been a question, like a gentle tune playing in the back of my mind. Am I saying that in order to emerge to this higher way of being we have to return to a spiritual way of living, an inner journey? Mine has brought me such an array of beautiful experiences it is only natural to want to share and to point people towards this path.

Through my own process, I have not become a practising Jew but I have stopped pushing it away and I have allowed the concertina to play its sonorous and emotive melodies, enabling me to embrace my whole story, not just the parts I fancy. In that spirit of wholeness it has been like a homecoming. However, I am not saying that this is the only way for there are many routes to the same destination. I am saying that it is the way that worked for me.

I lived, before my awakening, locked within the culture of secularism, an agreed consensus that was created for and by the ego mindset over the last 500 years. I made that leap of faith and understood how uncomfortable and illogical it feels to step out of the box. But, how else might we solve the crises we are facing? While we remain in the extremity of our minds, represented by the leaves on the trees, my constant question is, how will we reconcile our differences and come back to our hearts?

My next steps are all about embedding myself in my community to explore the conflict between the oppressor and the victim within, the crosses that each bear and hand down to their descendants; how we allowed Lilith's dissenting cry against inequality be replaced by Eve's consenting silence.

It is time to reinvent our story, or rediscover those that have been buried, like *The Hermetica*. Equipped with new and ancient narratives that speak and work in right relationship with Mother Earth, we can find our own direct way back to a G-d that embraces the whole of humanity, without exception.

Wherever I looked I came across the idea of the paradoxical nature of life, not realising that this was to be the learning, the gift. Simultaneously, the Kabbalah revealed to me that life is more about losing rather than finding oneself and that in the empty space, in the stillness, the answers flood in. When we return to our hearts we discover that everything resides there, the whole universe dancing on the end of a pin.

Whatever our fears, the paradox is that where the shadow is strong, the light is equally powerful. When we break through the pain barriers, the walls we have built around our hearts, we may find an all-encompassing G-d that speaks for and to everyone. Once we are back in the Garden of Eden, nothing will make sense as we discover what it means to live a life steeped in paradox.

Here is a wonderful quote from the book *Love Without End* by Glenda Green:

> 'Love is a gift, a miracle, a mystery ... The power of love is that it commands the zero point where time and space become one ... and resistance falls away. There, in the Holy Now, all duality is resolved into the miracle of paradox. By giving, you receive. By releasing, you attain. By forgiving you are forgiven. By doing nothing, all is done. By surrendering, all is conquered. This only happens in the presence of love.' [12]

I stand up, my Minotaur, who has been conspicuous by its absence for a while now, is moving around far in the depths of the petal. It's time and I need to find my mettle. I close my eyes and immediately sense myself at the top of one of the trees that has been growing in my beautiful petal of Strength. I recognise this place, metaphorically teetering on the flimsy top branches, nestled in the leaves. Once more, I remember my friend's words, 'we will be asked to choose between the shadow or the light' and

I make my choice. I will meet my Minotaur whichever I choose, but how I do that is up to me.

When we run away from our fears we are choosing the shadow, but if we can face them, they will be dissolved within the all-encompassing light. My need to work with reconciliation has shown me that conflict is not something to fear but a gift, a chance to grow and rise above differences so we can celebrate them. This will bring me back to that place in my heart, where all our hearts connect.

The journey will take years but I am prepared to go the distance, to make the pilgrimage to the field beyond right and wrong.

I clamber safely down, like a finger labyrinth it is a practice run for the real voyage. When I reach the bottom my Minotaur is waiting for me but not yet in view. We are going to enter the heart of the labyrinth together.

'Are you ready?'

'Yes, I believe I am,' I say, and it is a strong belief.

A light from nowhere seems to define the space and my Minotaur steps forward. Its huge body towers over me but it has a grace and agility I hadn't expected. Its form, whereas before it had been either frightening or emaciated, is fierce and had I not become acquainted with it throughout our time together, it would have terrified me. But now I can only see its majesty, its power, which in turn empowers me. My fears allayed, no hiding or shielding, I finally see the beauty in the beast.

EPILOGUE

THE GIFT

The six petals completed, and now sitting in the heart of the labyrinth itself, I am ready to receive the gift, the answer. It was always my wish that by the end of this journey I would have a clearer picture of myself than when I started. Although the way has not been without its obstacles I always hoped, at the outset, that I would be able to leave with a sense of completion that would reveal the next pilgrimage to me.

I take a moment to look around, the terrain here is beautiful and serene, the colours have a brilliance and the vibrancy is palpable. Gathering my thoughts while I remain in this enchanting energy, just breathing in the air fills me with a sense of awe and joy. The time spent here feels like a gift in itself but I know there is something here to consolidate, which will send me on my way.

I sit down, ready for the last process. My Minotaur is close by as I quiet my mind.

I sense that my task is simply to gather the loose threads, to hold them all in my hand, knowing that they will guide me out of the labyrinth and eventually form the rope that will hoist me up to the next stage of my journey. While I still don't know exactly what that entails, I do know that I need to prepare myself.

'So how are you going to do that, what will you take from this journey and carry with you?' I relax into the sound of the familiar voice that has accompanied me this far.

'What indeed?'

I pause to gather my thoughts and review my journey and how it has focused my scattered intentions.

My explorations have shown me how my life is a balancing act between opposites, my two Pisces fish swimming in opposite directions. I see myself as being both British and Jewish, white and non-white, privileged and oppressed, abundant and impoverished. I felt this was helping me see both sides of the many stories we tell.

It is my belief that our rejection of faith and all things spiritual has cast us adrift. We needed to anchor ourselves, so we built walls of protection around our heart, in the belief that they would keep us safe. However, we actually placed ourselves outside the walls, with G-d still safely within. The walls were simply mirroring our eviction from the garden.

Cut off from source, our world, limited by our egocentric view, became smaller and more frightening. We have separated ourselves from our divinity, the comforting and supportive embrace of the universal love within us all. This left us, having to navigate the hardships of the world we created, alone. As we gradually mislaid our soul purpose, our feelings of abundance and our ability to forgive ourselves for this loss, we have also created stories of disempowerment to keep us locked into this mindset. Yet, even when the stories have been discarded, they are still whispering through the echo chambers of our ancestors in the very cells of our bodies.

When we ignore our Minotaur, refrain from engaging in all the difficult aspects of our world, death as well as life, the dark as well as the light, we will remain cowering in the very corners of our mind, terrified of our shadow. Our inability to face what we have become has created an inner conflict with a destructive nature that knows no bounds.

I have wrestled with my own inner conflict and ancestral pain, and discovered that as a Jew I am both brown and white.

This showed me that we are all, in a sense, the embodiment of the transitions we have made as a race and it is my hope that we can learn to coexist with this duality. This fed my desire to explore what the ancients and the quantum physicists say: that we can be two things at once and that DNA is not fixed.

This is a journey, a mirror that we can all gaze into. It reflects back the complexity of emotions that we hold collectively, the hatred and the celebration, the abuse and the love that we feel about ourselves but are so quick to project onto others and also our wonderful, natural world. This has shaped our pilgrimage from paradise to paradox.

While we long to be free, to throw open the doors of the fortress in which we are confined, we are the ones holding both the locks and the keys. The main gateway is the wound itself, but the West lacks the compassion and the intuitive therapeutic and somatic processes required to open these doors. It is this wisdom, the people who have been systematically oppressed by the West, have had to hold onto or weave into their culture in order to survive. If we are going to learn these ways, the journey requires humility, and thankfully, I know many are already stepping onto the path.

I see our Hero's Journey of separation as an opportunity, whether we live in the spiritual heart of the world or not, whether we believe we are in a position of power or not. I feel our return is dependent on whether we make a stand for love or remain in the cycle of victimhood, continuing to oppress the 'other' as an outward projection of our inner pain.

I believe that we have all been 'chosen' by G-d, we each have a role to play, individually and collectively to be 'a light unto the nations.' If we, as a culture, view G-d through the small lens then G-d becomes like a chess player playing our lives like pawns and we see everyone around us as our competitors. If we see G-d through the wide lens then G-d becomes the chessboard itself and we are both the player and the pawns weaving our lives together in a magical journey of destiny and creativity.

If we can bring ourselves to recognise that it is our own inner conflict that is creating our destruction, then might we choose a different destiny? It will take great strength – to reverse the idea that the mind has to have power over the heart – to ensure the necessary changes are made when so many resist and refuse to act.

When I learned that turning away rather than facing the pain was the error here and that to sin was to only miss the mark, regaining our inner strength seemed possible.

This is my call to action, a need to blow my bugle, to summon all dissenters or silenced participants, everyone who feels drawn to carry the banner of reclaiming our love in a radical way. I want to join those who are ready to face their inner conflict, recognise when they step into judgement and when they put up walls between themselves and the conflict that needs challenging. Then the Minotaur will be alive and well in our world, empowering us rather than oppressing us.

My sense that as we are all victims in some way, disconnected from our inner wisdom, this means that we are all potentially part of the problem. Knowing this can put the power back in our hands, giving us the opportunity to choose to turn this around and be part of the solution. Then we can face our demons, stop seeing the problem as someone else's and start tackling the issues individually and as a community.

My moon analogy keeps coming back to me, and I am reminded of the movie *Apollo 13*. Three men in a rocket on their way to the moon, a real life disaster that was diverted against all odds. I believe that with the combined effort and determination of a community, we can problem solve our way out of the mess we've got ourselves into, if we set our hearts to it.

This is a huge task, but I sense that as the pace gathers, those who are also sounding their sirens and choosing to come to the table will, like a chorus, begin to be heard. I hope you will consider your place here too.

It is time to leave, bring my gift out into the world; a process of reconciliation that I will grow from my learning here. I see my Minotaur is already waiting for me, ready to revisit all the stages of this journey and take the long path out of the labyrinth. I sense that each petal, representing our many divisions, has a purpose, a way to bring us home, away from the path of self-destruction we appear to be on.

We encounter the last petal first, the petal of Strength. I see on the ground next to me there is a golden thread. I hadn't noticed it before but now it is there as clear as day. It is an invitation. The thread (Ariadne's gift to Theseus as he made his exit after slaying the Minotaur) will show us the way even though there is only one path, this labyrinth being a unicursal structure, but still I take it up gladly.

Once in my hand, the energy pulsing through my fingers, I sense I am treading in the footsteps of many who have gone before me. I keep a tight hold, trusting that I will not be led astray. Courage, the rage that is stirring in my heart, fires me up with the knowledge that with every step I take I have my whole ancestral lineage guiding me.

I have travelled from paradise to paradox in the knowledge that they are one and the same .

Feeling empowered and strengthened by this, and knowing that healing is all about feeling, I am ready to take the next step.

Extricating myself from the extremities of my mind, the leaves of my tree, I reach in to connect with the twig that is clutching this group of leaves.

Here I arrive at the next petal, the petal of Forgiveness and there is another piece of thread. Holding the two strands together I feel my energy expand as I step down to the branch that is bearing the twig I am willingly letting go of. The sense of forgiveness in myself feels palpable and I arrive in the next petal.

The petal of Abundance is now overflowing with the gifts from Mother Nature and I breathe it in with gratitude. The gold of the thread catches my eye in the undergrowth and I pick it up and put it in my hand. I play with them between my fingers and it feels good to bring these three threads together. My body begins to relax and breathe, feeling more in tune with my surroundings than ever before, the love from my connection to myself, those that have come before and the natural world, running through my veins; I feel expansive.

As I slip down the branch to one of the three great branches of my tree I feel I am entering the very base of my brain, where all thoughts are no longer my own. I enter the petal of Service and it offers me the fourth golden thread and as it makes contact with the other three somehow my personal gifts feel more real, their purpose more valid. My step gains pace as my desire to fulfil what before seemed just like dreams, beat more powerfully in me.

Like on a helter-skelter I slide down into my heart, my zero-point, where feelings of separation are just a distant memory. I can feel into the core of my being, down to the roots and into the soil that feeds me.

The last two threads, of Surrender and Faith, slip into my palm like friends and altogether they feel almost like a rope that is strong and tugging at me to get into motion. The journey out of the labyrinth is joyous as I feel complete, fully equipped to make my way towards my next pilgrimage, which at the moment is still unknown. This will be the content of my next book and I see it lying behind a mist, like the fog around St Catherine's Chapel.

I don't feel any fear about saying that I don't know what it will entail or look like. I just trust that these six threads will guide me as I learn to weave them together and formulate a way of taking my ideas of reconciliation into the world.

'Easy to say.' My friend is ever present.

'Yes, I know, but it sounds great doesn't it? Hundreds of pitfalls ahead of me, but I'm learning that's all part of the fun, no? And just as I started this journey, it's all about setting good intentions. No point starting at base camp, aim high, I say.'

I hear what sounds like chuckling.

'And I know you'll keep pulling me up whenever I overreach myself.'

I know we're done and it's really time to leave.

My Minotaur is accompanying me and not just out of the labyrinth, this majestic animal, rather than being the frightening beast that I dare not look at, is now my companion, the part of me that can stand up and question, face life, face death and look conflict in the eye. That's what I believe, and I know I will have to prove that these are not just words but my new reality.

I'D LOVE TO HEAR FROM YOU!

If you would like to discuss any of the matters in this book, keep in touch about book 1 and book 3 in the trilogy or wish to find out more about my other work – performances, journeys, meditations or workshops – please visit www.keystothegoldencity.com

My new album, *Beauty in the Beast - a Musical Journey into the Labyrinth*, is now available on CD, as an accompaniment to this book and the lyrics at the beginning of each chapter.
To order your copy, please visit www.keystothegoldencity.com or www.vickiburke.bandcamp.com

You can also follow me on Facebook, Twitter, SoundCloud, or my Blogspot: Journey to the Golden City.

END NOTES

PROLOGUE

[1] Schrödinger's cat is a paradoxical experiment devised by the Austrian physicist Erwin Schrödinger in 1935. It offers the idea that a cat, whilst hidden inside a box, can be either alive or dead, depending on what has occurred inside. The answer is only known when the box is opened and the observer brings one of the possibilities into play, simply by witnessing it. Before this, both states are possible. (Wikipedia).

It is interesting how people are taking this literally rather than as an analogy once again and questioning this theory. To me this is about perception not hard and fast states of being. Do we experience atoms as particles or waves, are we physical beings or spiritual? We are of course both but that is dependent on who is participating in the supposition.

CHAPTER 2

[2] The hundredth monkey effect is a hypothetical phenomenon in which a new behaviour or idea is spread rapidly by unexplained means from one group to all related groups once a critical number of members of one group exhibit the new behaviour or acknowledge the new idea. The behaviour was said to propagate even to groups that are physically separated and have no apparent means of communicating with each other. (Wikipedia).

CHAPTER 4

[3] *Book of Isaiah* (Isaiah 42:6).

[4] The word 'chosen' should here, as in the Bible, carry the sense of being separated rather than being favoured. From the *Gospel of Thomas* notes by Hugh McGregor Ross p 107.

[5] Ho'oponopono is a Hawaiian practice of reconciliation and forgiveness.

CHAPTER 6

[6] Gibran, Kahlil. *The Prophet.* p 34.

[7] Somatics describes any practice that uses the mind–body connection to help you survey your internal self and listen to signals your body sends about areas of pain, discomfort or imbalance. https://www.healthline.com/health/somatics.

[8] The torus is a core level sacred geometry form. This image graphs the process by which all energy, when it is correctly aligned, continually is cycling, up and down and around, between spirit and matter. https://www.crystal-life.com

In geometry, a torus (plural tori) is a surface of revolution generated by revolving a circle in three-dimensional space about an axis that is coplanar with the circle. https://en.wikipedia.org/wiki/Torus.

[9] I learned in David Baddiel's *Jews Don't Count* that 'there is an online thing … a satirical hashtag … often placed by feminists after something critical of the patriarchy.' p 105.

[10] Karen L King, *The Gospel of Mary of Magdala*, p 76.

[11] Located deep and medially within the temporal lobes of the brain's cerebrum in complex vertebrates, including humans. Shown to perform a primary role in the processing of memory, decision-making and emotional responses (including fear, anxiety and aggression). https://en.wikipedia.org/wiki/Amygdala.

[12] Green, Glenda. *Love Without End*, p.358

BIBLIOGRAPHY

Abdulrazzak, Hassan. *Love, Bombs and Apples* (play). Bloomsbury Publishing. 2016.

Al-Raee, Nabil. *The Siege* (play).The Freedom Theatre, Jenin, 2015.

Brecht, B. *Threepenny Opera* (play). 1928.

Brock, Rita Nakashima, Parker, Rebecca Ann. *Saving Paradise*. Beacon Press, 2009.

Burke, Vicki. *Journey to the Golden City*. Self-published by Matador of Troubador Publishing Ltd, 2017.
Burke, Vicki. *Return to the Golden City* (play). 2014. Available from author.

Coelho, Paulo. *The Alchemist*. London: HarperCollins Publishers, 1998.

Divine, John the. *The Book of Revelation*, Arcturus Publishing Ltd, 2011.

van Fessem, Johanna. *Walking in the Light*. English translation published in Glastonbury: Dancing Mountain, 2013.

Freke, Timothy, Gandy, Peter. *The Hermetica: The Lost Wisdom of the Pharaohs*. JP Tarcher/Putnam, 1999.

Gibran, Kahlil. *The Prophet*. Alfred A. Knopf, 1923.

Green, Glenda. *Love Without End*. Spiritis Publishing, 1999.

King, Karen L. *The Gospel of Mary of Magdala*. Polebridge Press, USA, 2003.

Kornfield, Jack. *After The Ecstasy, The Laundry*. Rider of Ebury Publishing, 2000.

Leitch, Yuri, ed. *Secrets and Signs of the Glastonbury Zodiac* (anthology). Avalonian Aeon Publications, 2014.

Pappe, Ilan. *The Ethnic Cleansing of Palestine.* One World Publications, 2007.

Philp, Chrissy. *The Golden City.* Self-published, 1996.

Puzo, Mario. *The Godfather.* GP Putnam's Sons, 1969.

Shakespeare, W. *Romeo and Juliet.* 1591–95.

Ustinov, P. *Romanoff and Juliet* (play). English Theatre Guild, 1957.

Walsh, Neale Donald. *Conversations with God.* London: Hodder and Stoughton, 1996.

FILMOGRAPHY

Beyond Right and Wrong. Spottiswoode, R. 2012, Article 19 Films, cinema.

Sliding Doors. Howitt, P. Miramax Films, 1998, cinema.

Two-Sided Story. Ben-Mayor, Tor. 2012, DVD.

West Side Story. Wise, R and Robbins, J. United Artists, 1961, cinema.

DISCOGRAPHY

Leonard Bernstein (music), Stephen Sondheim (lyrics) 'Somewhere'. *West Side Story*, United Artists, 1961.

David Bowie. 'Quicksand'. *Hunky Dory*, RCA, 1971.

Vicki Burke. 'Keys to the Golden City', Shine Records, 2017.

Vicki Burke. 'Sulha'. *Beauty In The Beast*, Shine Records, 2021.

Pink Floyd. 'Comfortably Numb', *The Wall*, Harvest, 1980.

John Williams. 'Theme from Schindler's List'. *Schindler's List: Original Motion Picture Soundtrack*, MCA, 1994.

FURTHER REFERENCE

The Alchemical Journey John Wadsworth https://www.facebook.com/alchemicaljourney

Satish Kumar https://www.resurgence.org/satish-kumar/

Frome Friends of Palestine https://www.facebook.com/groups/1429491273980296

Jo Berry https://buildingbridgesforpeace.org

Peace One Day Jeremy Gilley https://peaceoneday.org

Mike Brecker https://www.facebook.com/groups/michael.brecker/

Penny Brohn Cancer Care Centre https://www.pennybrohn.org.uk

St Stephen's Church, Bristol, UK https://www.saint-stephens.com

Sulha Project https://www.facebook.com/sulhapp/

The Freedom Theatre https://www.thefreedomtheatre.org

Peter Woolf – The Woolf Within. A Restorative Justice video available on Youtube

TreeSisters https://treesisters.org